JOB SAVVY

HOW TO BE
A SUCCESS AT WORK

LaVerne Ludden, Ed.D.

Publisher: J. Michael Farr
Project Director: Spring Dawn Reader
Editor: Sara Hall
Cover Design: Dean Johnson Design Group
Interior Design: Spring Dawn Reader

JOB SAVVY—HOW TO BE A SUCCESS AT WORK
©1992, JIST Works, Inc., Indianapolis, IN

Ordering Information: An order form has been provided at the end of this book containing other related materials.

JIST Works, Inc.
720 North Park Avenue • Indianapolis, IN 46202-3431
Phone: **(317) 264-3720** • FAX: **(317) 264-3709**

ISBN: 0-942784-79-0

About This Book

This is a book about keeping a job and getting ahead. Based on research into what employers actually look for in the people who succeed or fail, *Job Savvy* is designed to develop critical job survival skills, increase productivity, and improve job satisfaction and success. Using a workbook approach, many in-the-book activities are provided to reinforce key points and develop new job survival skills and plans. The narrative is easy to read and informative using good graphic design, many examples, checklists, case studies, and section summaries.

Why People Need to Improve Their Basic Job Skills

The years ahead are projected to be a time of labor market opportunity and challenge for most workers. Some of these trends include:

- Many new and existing jobs will require higher levels of technical skills.
- The amount of education and training required for jobs will increase.
- Employers will expect their employees to be more productive and obtain better results in more complex jobs.
- More job and career changes are anticipated for the average worker.

All of these changes will require a person who is better prepared than most workers have been in the past. The biggest need, according to most employers and labor market experts, is for workers to have good "basic" skills. These include having basic academic skills, the ability to communicate, to adapt to new situations, and to solve problems. While these and other related skills are not technical skills in the traditional sense, they have everything to do with long-term success on the job. And this is what this book is about.

A Different Point of View

You will find numerous references in *Job Savvy* to the studies and research of psychologists, sociologists and other labor market professionals. Yet this is NOT an academic book. Instead, this information has been used to form the basis for a practical and useful handbook for a working person — or one who soon plans to enter the world of work. Many employers have asked for such a book to give them a tool to encourage their new workers to succeed on the job. And because the author has been both an employer and a trainer of new employees, he brings a unique and helpful point of view that will bridge the gap between an employer's and an employee's expectations. The result of this is increased job savvy where, we believe, both will win.

> ### A Parable
> *An explorer was once asked what he most disliked about the wilderness. "Is it the wolves?" "No," he replied, "it's the mosquitoes." In a similar way, many people fail on the job as a result of the little problems, not the big ones. This book will help you identify and avoid both, so you can be the best employee you can be.*

TABLE OF CONTENTS

©1992, JIST Works, Inc. • Indianapolis, Indiana

Chapter One

Understanding the Employment Relationship

GREAT EXPECTATIONS

Whenever you start a new adventure, you have expectations about what will happen. Starting a new job is one such adventure. You may expect the job to provide you with opportunities for a highly successful career or you may just expect it to help pay for a new car. Research shows that the more realistic your expectations are about the job, the more likely it is that you will enjoy it.[1] This chapter tells you what employers expect from you as an employee and what you should expect from your employer.

What Does My Employer Want Anyway?

To understand what employers expect from the people they hire, put yourself in their place. Suppose that you own a business like a hardware store or a restaurant, or imagine that you are a supply supervisor for a large hospital. Now answer the following questions.

1. What are some important things that your organization must do to run productively and efficiently?

_____

_____

_____

_____

_____

2. What skills would you want your employees to have?

_____

_____

_____

_____

_____

Compare your answers to question 2 with those found in the "Workplace Basics" study described below.

Workplace Basics

The "Workplace Basics" study was conducted by the American Society for Training and Development (ASTD) to find out what basic skills employers think are needed by employees. The study found that most employers want their employees to possess what are termed the "workplace basics."[2] The seven basic skills are:

1. **Knowing How to Learn.** The concept of lifelong learning is now in common use among business people. Employers spend approximately $30 billion dollars annually for employee training. Another $180 billion is invested in informal or on-the-job training. Employees who do not know how to learn will be unable to take advantage of this investment and will soon find themselves obsolete.

2. **Reading, Writing, and Computation.** People who are weak in these skills will have trouble learning and will not function well in most jobs. The Hudson Institute predicts that the average education required for a job by the year 2000 will be 13.5 years, compared with the current level of 12.8 years. That prediction is based on the assumption that present occupations will require no more education than is currently the case. A slight trend—showing many occupations increasing their educational requirements—is evidenced.

3. **Listening and Oral Communication.** "The average person spends 8.4 percent of communications time writing, 13.3 percent reading, 23 percent speaking, and 55 percent listening." ("Workplace Basics: The Skills Employers Want," American Society for Training and Development.) Communication thus becomes at least as critical to success on the job as the 3 R's (above).

4. **Adaptability.** Organizations must be flexible to adapt and keep pace with advances in technology, changes in the marketplace, and new management practices. Employees who are creative problem- solvers are essential in today's business world.

5. **Personal Management.** This category covers a variety of skills: self-esteem, goal-setting/motivation, and personal/career development. Self-esteem is necessary for employees to take pride in their work. Goal-setting helps motivate employees to achieve stated objectives. Finally, employees must know how to advance within an organization and what opportunities lie outside their present employer's operation. As more businesses move toward the use of self-management and participative management, these skills will become increasingly necessary.

6. **Group Effectiveness.** Individualism is a thing of the past in most jobs. It is far more important that workers understand and practice teamwork, negotiation, and interpersonal skills. People who understand how to work effectively in groups are the foundation of modern organizations that build successful enterprises.

7. **Influence.** Each employee must establish their own influence in order to successfully contribute ideas to an organization. It is frustrating to have a great idea that would improve the employer's operation but not know how to get it accepted. Employees must understand the organizational structure and informal networks in order to implement new ideas or to complete some tasks.

Employee Skills Checklist

Look at the following checklist and rank in order from 1 (most important) to 10 (least important) the employee skills you believe are most important to the success of your organization.

____Work habits

____Dependability

____Desire to get ahead

____Quality of work

____Concern for productivity

____Responsibility

____Ability to read and apply printed matter

____Attitudes toward company and employer

____Ability to follow instructions

____Ability to write and speak effectively

Dependability vs. Reliability

The definition of these two words is very similar. When we use these words in the world of work, they usually have two slightly different meanings. Dependability means that you will be on time and at work every day. It also means that you will notify your supervisor when you are unable to be at work. Reliability means that you will follow through with a job. When your supervisor asks you to do a job, you will get it done, and look for things to do when you have completed assigned tasks.

Listed below are the same skills you ranked from 1 to 10 in the Employee Skills Checklist. Explain why you think each of these skills is important in making an organization work as it should.

Work habits

_____

_____

_____

Dependability

_____

_____

_____

Desire to get ahead

_____

_____

_____

Quality of work

_____

_____

_____

Concern for productivity

_____

_____

_____

Responsibility

_____

_____

_____

Ability to read and apply printed matter

_____

_____

_____

Attitudes toward company and employer

_____

_____

_____

Ability to follow instructions

_____

_____

_____

Ability to write and speak effectively

_____

_____

_____

Employer Expectations

Business Basics

Let's look at what you have learned from the exercises just completed. In the first exercise, you listed those things that an employer needs to run a productive and efficient organization. Three essential things you might have included on your list are:

1. **Provide a Product or Service of High Quality.** Consumers want quality in whatever they buy. No one will buy a car that falls apart after the first 5,000 miles or go back to a restaurant that took an hour to serve their food. Organizations today are putting a great deal of emphasis on quality. The U.S. Government recognizes companies for their emphasis on quality by awarding them the Malcolm Baldridge National Quality Award.[3] This award was established because of our country's awareness of the importance of quality if we are to be competitive in a world economy.

2. **Satisfy the Customer's Needs and Wants.** Even though an organization sells good products and services, it can still fail. It is important that customers are treated well and given what they want. An organization depends on the goodwill of its customers. If customers are pleased with the products purchased or service received, they will continue to do business with that organization and even recommend it to other people. Think about this. If you walk into a store to buy a television and the salesperson is not helpful and knowledgeable about televisions, you will probably be upset. Chances are high that you will leave the store without buying anything and may not return to that store again.

3. **Make a Profit.** Product quality and customer satisfaction have to be provided at a cost which allows the business to make a profit. All businesses must make a profit or there is no reason for the owners or stockholders to continue the operation. They could invest their money elsewhere and receive a higher rate of return on their investment. For example, if they simply put their money in a savings account they might earn 5 to 9 percent interest.

Even government and nonprofit agencies must provide satisfactory service for less than the amount of money they have in their budget. Nonprofit agencies must earn enough money to pay all of their expenses. However, they can't distribute earnings that add up to more than their expenses to stockholders or others involved in the operation of the organization. Many hospitals, counseling centers, social service agencies and private schools are operated as nonprofit organizations. Government and nonprofit agencies are expected to operate as efficiently as profit-making businesses.

Profit

What is a profit? It is the amount of money an organization has left after paying all its expenses. The money that an organization earns through sales or services is called income. All bills the organization pays are called expenses. The profit is calculated by subtracting expenses from income. Profits belong to the owner, partners, or stockholders of an organization. Some people wonder why organizations should make a profit. A profit is the compensation business owners receive for risking their money in a commercial venture. Often owners will take money from their profit and reinvest it in the organization by buying new equipment, opening new facilities, hiring new workers, etc. This investment of profit creates a healthy economy. Some business owners have profit-sharing programs that distribute a share of profits to all employees as a reward for their hard work.

An employer expects all employees to help the organization accomplish the three essentials of a successful operation. You will be expected to work hard, help when asked, please customers, and do it for a wage that allows the organization to make a profit and stay in business.

Employee Skills

This exercise is meant to help you understand that employers are looking for employees who have more skills than just those needed to do a specific job, such as the typing and filing skills necessary in a secretarial job. There is a broader base of skills that employers want you to have. These are called adaptive or self-management skills, and they help you adjust to your workplace. For example, getting along with co-workers and listening to your supervisor's instructions are adaptive skills. These self-management skills will be explored more fully in chapter 6.

A list of skills employers want employees to have was compiled from a survey of employers by The Advisory Council for Technical-Vocational Education in Texas.[4] Employers were asked to identify areas they believed employees needed to improve. The order in which employers ranked these 10 items is shown on the following page.

---

10 Self-Managment Skills Employers Want to See in Their Employees

1. Concern for productivity
2. Pride of craftsmanship and quality of work
3. Responsibility and ability to follow through on assigned tasks
4. Dependability
5. Work habits
6. Attitudes toward company and employer
7. Ability to write and speak effectively
8. Ability to read and apply printed matter
9. Ability to follow instructions
10. Ambition/motivation/desire to get ahead

Ask yourself how many of these skills you have demonstrated in the past. Think of ways that you can practice these on your job and impress your employer. Remember, your employer hired you for your skills. Your value as an employee will increase when you apply these attitudes and skills on the job.

Applying What You've Learned

The following situations are common for most employers. Read the following case studies and answer the questions based on what you have learned about employer expectations.

Case Study 1

Tom takes orders at a fast food restaurant. He has worked at the restaurant for three weeks and believes he deserves a raise. After his shift ends, Tom talks with his supervisor, Janet, and tells her that he feels he deserves a raise.

1. If you were Janet, what would you tell Tom?

   _____

   _____

2. Why would you tell Tom this?

   _____

   _____

Case Study 2

Angel works as a file clerk for a large insurance company. As her supervisor, you told her to go to the supply room for a box of new file folders. Later you find Angel sitting at her desk filing her nails. When you ask, "Why aren't you working?", Angel replies, "I ran out of file folders."

1. What would you say to Angel?

    _____

    _____

2. What skill(s) does she need to improve?

    _____

    _____

What Should You Expect?

Everyone works for different reasons. Most of us have several reasons for working. Your motivation and interest in a job will depend on your reasons for working and how well the job satisfies your needs.

1. List your reasons for working below. You may think of money right away. Go ahead and list money if that is one of your reasons. However, think about the other reasons you work.

    Reasons for Working

    _____   _____

    _____   _____

    _____   _____

2. Think about the jobs you've had. What did you like about each job? What did you dislike?

    Likes

    _____   _____

    _____   _____

    Dislikes

    _____   _____

    _____   _____

    _____   _____

3. How do you expect an employer to treat you? What are things you want in return for the work you do?

My Expectations

_____   _____

_____   _____

_____   _____

What I Want

_____   _____

_____   _____

_____   _____

Reasons for Working

You can't expect every job to satisfy all of your expectations and values. Many people work at jobs they don't want until they can get the education or experience necessary to start the career they do want. For example, you may work as a stock clerk for the opportunity to later become store manager. Sometimes it is necessary to make sacrifices while you work toward the job you want. Few jobs provide complete satisfaction. You must determine your most important expectations and values, then evaluate what each job offers.

There are a number of sources to use to help you understand what American workers consider the most important job values and expectations. Richard Plunkett reports on a 1986 poll taken by Louis Harris and Associates that questioned 1,250 employees in the U.S. and Canada.[5] Employees were asked to rank those things that were very important in their jobs. The results are listed below.

Items Ranked Highest	Percent of Employees (%)
A challenging job	82
Good benefits	80
Good pay	74
Free exchange of information	74
Chance to make significant contributions	74
The right to privacy	62

Plunkett reports on another poll taken by Media General-Associated Press. In this poll, workers were asked to give the reason they liked their work. The reasons given are shown on the following page.

Reason Workers Like Their Work	Percent of Workers (%)
The work itself	32
People at work	23
Money	12
Hours	7
Benefits	6
Boss	3
Other	17

In his book on human relations, Andrew DuBrin suggests there are external factors and internal causes that affect job satisfaction.[6] When you compare the lists below, you will see that there are fewer external factors controlled by the employer than are controlled by you. To a large degree, you are responsible for the way you feel about your job. You can increase your job satisfaction by focusing on the internal causes and rewards of what you are doing.

External Factors	Internal Causes
■ Mentally challenging work	■ Interest in the work itself
■ Reasonable physical demands	■ Work fitting one's job values
■ Meaningful rewards	■ Positive self-image
■ Contact with customer/end user	■ Good personal adjustment
■ Helpful co-workers and superiors	■ Positive expectations about the job
	■ A feeling of self-esteem reinforced by the job optimism and flexibility

In addition to the things you personally expect from an employer, there are certain requirements the federal and state governments place on an employer. The following section reviews these requirements.

Understanding Your Rights

There are several things that an employer is required by law to do for employees. Listed below are the main things that the government requires of an employer. It is important to understand that these explanations are very general. Labor law is changing as new laws are passed by federal and state governments. It is further complicated by court decisions as to how these laws should be interpreted.

The following information is only intended as a review of what employers should do. If you think your employer isn't following the law, respectfully discuss this with your supervisor. If you aren't satisfied with the answers from your supervisor or other management personnel, then contact an elected official such as a representative or senator, the mayor's office or the governor's office to find out what organization you must contact to get your questions answered.

Laws and Regulations in the Workplace

There are a number of laws and regulations that affect workers on the job. Since it is difficult to provide a summary of all state regulations, you will find that only the federal regulations have been listed with each topic.

Fair Wage

- **Fair Labor Standards Act (FLSA)** — Governs minimum wage and child labor laws.

- **The Work Hours Act of 1962** — Extends the application of FLSA, including provisions for paying employees time and a half.

- **The Equal Pay Act of 1972** — Established equal payment for overtime regardless of gender.

- **Walsh-Healy Act** — Governs minimum wage to be paid for federal government suppliers of equipment, materials and supplies.

- **Davis-Bacon Act** — Governs minimum wage to be paid by contractors for federally funded construction projects.

Most employers are required to pay the minimum wage. One study concluded that approximately 92 percent of all employers must pay the minimum wage.[7] This wage will vary according to federal regulations. Some states have minimum wage laws that may require employers to pay a higher wage than the federal minimum. Research the answers to the questions below.

1. What is the minimum wage in your state?

_____

2. What is the current federal minimum wage?

_____

Equal Opportunity

- **Age Discrimination in Employment Act of 1967** — Prohibits firms with 20 or more employees from discriminating against workers 40 years of age and older.

- **Equal Employment Opportunity Act of 1972** — Prohibits firms with 20 or more employees from discriminating against workers because of their race, color, sex, religion, or national origin.

- **Pregnancy Discrimination Act of 1978** — Requires that pregnant women be entitled to benefits related to sick leave that would be given for other medical reasons.

- **Vocational Rehabilitation Act of 1973** — Prohibits employers with federal contracts of $2,500 or greater from discriminating against persons because of any physical or mental impairment.
- **Vietnam Era Veterans' Readjustment Act of 1974** — Prohibits firms with federal contracts of $10,000 or more from discriminating against Vietnam era veterans.

Your employer cannot discriminate in pay promotions, training or in any other way because of your race, sex, age, handicap, national origin or religion.

1. How would you pursue a question about discrimination?

_____

_____

_____

_____

Child Labor Laws

Employers are expected to abide by child labor laws. These laws prevent employers from employing anyone under the age of 14. Youth aged 14 to 15 years are limited in the number of hours and time of day they can work, and are excluded from work in manufacturing, mining, or hazardous jobs. Workers ages 16 and 17 are also excluded from employment in hazardous jobs. Employers are responsible for obtaining proof of age from the young people they hire. This is the reason many employers ask for a work permit as proof of age. High school counselors can advise youth about how to obtain a work permit.

1. Are you under 18? If so, what restrictions will you have because of your age?

_____

_____

_____

_____

Worker Safety

- **Occupational Safety and Health Act of 1970 (OSHA)** — Places several requirements on employers to provide safe working conditions for employees and protects from dismissal employees who report unsafe working conditions.
- **Hazard Communication Standard (an addition to OSHA)** — Prescribes a system for informing employees about health hazards and how to respond to exposure from such hazards.

There are many federal and state laws governing employee safety. Employers are expected to provide a work area that is both safe and clean. Any equipment that is operated should have protective guards. Employers must make sure that you wear proper safety equipment such as eye protectors, hard hats, steel-toed shoes, etc. You are also to be informed about any hazardous materials that you may work with, as well as what to do in case you are exposed to any hazardous materials. Again, youth under 18 years of age are restricted from working in any hazardous occupation.

1. What organization in your state reviews safety conditions in the workplace?

_____

Labor Relations

- **Wagner Act of 1935** — Guarantees employees the right to organize and participate in union activities.
- **Taft-Hartley Act of 1947** — Balances the rights of employers and unions.
- **Landrum-Griffin Act of 1957** — Guarantees union members certain rights within the union itself.

Employers are required by federal and some state laws to allow you to participate in lawful union activity. While there are laws to protect your participation in such activities, some employers may try to find another way to fire you for such participation. Carefully check with other employees to find out what they see as the benefits and drawbacks of joining a local union.

Several states have a right-to-work law. This means you aren't required to join a union that may exist at your employer's place of business. However, if you live in a state without this provision, you may still be required to pay union dues, because you benefit from the collective bargaining. Union dues vary, and are usually handled as automatic deductions from your paycheck.

1. Is there a union where you work?

_____

2. If so, what are the requirements for joining?

_____

_____

_____

_____

_____

3. How much are the union dues?

_____

4. Does your state have a right-to-work law?

_____

Fair Treatment

- **Worker Adjustment and Retraining Notification Act (WARN)** — Requires employers to provide 60 days advance warning for major layoffs or plant closings.

The federal government requires that certain employers give a 60-day warning for plant closings or mass layoffs.[8] If you work for such an employer, you should receive this advance warning.

Employment-at-Will is a legal term that means an employer can fire you at any time for any reason, but the termination cannot be in violation of federal or state law. The application of this concept has changed over the years by many state courts and in some cases by state legislatures. The "wrongful discharge" concept has begun to diminish the application of employment-at-will. According to the wrongful discharge concept, an employee should only be dismissed for "just cause." This places the burden of proof on the employer to show that the employee has done something serious enough to justify termination. The law related to dismissals varies from state to state and is undergoing a great deal of change. The only way one can be sure they were unfairly dismissed by an employer is to obtain the services of an attorney. However, it is often simply not worth the time to bother pursuing an unjust dismissal. It is frequently better to get on with your life; go out and find an employer who will really appreciate you and your skills.

1. What are the laws in your state that apply to the discipline and dismissal of an employee?

   _____

   _____

   _____

   _____

   _____

Resolving Employee Rights Issues

Knowledge of your rights as an employee is important. You need to be aware of how you should expect to be treated by your employer. However, there may be some employers who are not familiar with these laws or do not strictly follow them. You must determine how important you feel the problem is before you discuss it with your supervisor. Employees who constantly question possible violations of laws, policies, and procedures may be viewed as trouble makers. Your employment with an organization may be quite short if you are pegged as a "trouble maker." Should you decide to pursue any matter dealing with employee rights, follow the guidelines on the next page.

- Discuss the problem with your supervisor and ask them to correct the situation. When you talk with your supervisor, always approach the conversation in a respectful manner. Keep in mind that you may not correctly understand the situation. Give your supervisor an opportunity to explain why the problem may not be as serious as you think.

- If the supervisor doesn't correct the problem or you feel the explanation is inadequate, contact the personnel office or the owner. (Personnel handbooks usually describe the process you should follow when appealing a supervisor's actions.) Discuss your concerns and how they may be satisfied. Always do this in a polite and non-threatening manner. Be aware that your relationship with your supervisor may be negatively affected by this action.

- If the company doesn't correct the problem, you may want to contact the government agency responsible for seeing that the law is enforced. Your employer may fire you for this unless a specific law exists that protects you from such an action.

Whenever you approach a government agency to file a complaint, you will find that the follow-through requires a great deal of your time. It is necessary to meet with government officials to explain the problem. You may be required to testify at formal hearings. It is necessary to balance out the time requirements and pressures that are a part of such formal complaints against the benefits of having an employer change its illegal practices.

Applying What You've Learned

People work for many reasons. The following two cases describe jobs and working conditions at the jobs. Tell what you would like and dislike about each of these jobs.

Case Study 1

Kim works for a manufacturing company. The wages are not as high as those at similar local manufacturing companies. The other workers are friendly and helpful. Whenever someone has a problem, everyone helps out. The supervisor is a hard worker and pushes everyone to produce a high quality product as quickly as possible. The supervisor is easy to talk to and will normally listen to questions and complaints made by employees. Kim is often asked to work overtime. It is not unusual to work six days a week.

Likes

_____   _____

_____   _____

_____   _____

Dislikes

_____   _____

_____   _____

_____   _____

Case Study 2

Jackson is employed as a hospital nurse. The pay and fringe benefits are very good. There are often changes made in hospital procedures that Jackson doesn't find out about until they are to be put into practice. Jackson reports to a supervisor that is not very friendly and doesn't talk much about anything other than work. Other workers are cooperative but do not get together outside the hospital.

Likes

_____   _____

_____   _____

_____   _____

Dislikes

_____   _____

_____   _____

_____   _____

Summary

Your relationship with an employer is built upon three important concepts. First, you must understand the reason the employer is in business and respect his need to make the organization productive and profitable. Remember that the employer isn't in business just to provide you with a job. Second, you need to understand why you want to work and look for those things connected with your job that satisfy your reasons for working. You will be happier and do a better job when you realize that your job is meeting many of your needs. Third, a relationship of mutual respect between you and your employer is necessary. The employer may be required by law to behave toward you in a certain way. Many employers will want to do much more. You need to respect the employer's reasons for policies and decisions that affect you. Always try to resolve any misunderstandings in a positive manner.

Chapter One Endnotes

1. G. Leveto and J. Aplin, "Individual Expectation: Relationships to Attitudes, Perceptions and Intent to Turnover", *Proceedings of the 21st Annual Meeting of the Midwest Academy of Management*, (1978), 134-142.

2. Anthony P. Carnevale, Leila J. Gainer, and Ann S. Meltzer, "Workplace Basics: The Skills Employers Want", *American Society for Training and Development*, (U.S. Department of Labor, 1988).

3. Patricia A. Galagan, "David T. Kearns: A CEO's View of Training," *Training and Development Journal*, vol. 44(5), 41- 50.

4. "Qualities Employers Like and Dislike in Job Applicants: Final Report of Statewide Employer Survey," *The Advisory Council for Technical-Vocational Education in Texas*, (Austin, Texas, 1975).

5. Richard W. Plunkett, *Supervision: The Direction of People at Work*, (Allyn and Bacon, Boston, Mass., 1989), 164.

6. Andrew J. Dubrin, *Human Relations: A Job Oriented Approach*, (Prentice Hall, Englewood Cliffs, 1988), 74-76.

7. Sheldon I. London, *Understand Employee Regulations*, (London Publishing Company, Washington, D.C., 1988), 1.

8. "Worker Adjustment and Retraining Act (WARN)," (U.S. Department of Labor, 1989).

Chapter Two

Your First Day on the Job

Avoiding Those New Job Blues

It is very important for you to make a good impression your first day on the job. The impression you make on your supervisor and co-workers will have an effect on your future relationship with them. The first day can be confusing and difficult because you have a great deal to remember. This confusion can make it tough to create that positive first impression. However, you can reduce the confusion by knowing what to expect during the first day and being prepared.

The first day on the job will differ from one organization to another, but some things are the same. Here are some of the first day activities that will probably take place in most organizations.

- **Reporting to Work.** In larger organizations you will probably report to the personnel or human resources office. Smaller companies may have you report to the office manager or directly to your new supervisor.

- **Orientation.** Most organizations with more than 100 employees will provide some type of orientation training for new employees.[1] The purpose of orientation is to introduce you to the organization, take care of necessary paperwork and review policies and benefits.

- **Job Introduction.** You will usually receive some type of introduction to the job you will be doing. This task is often conducted by the supervisor.

This chapter will review what to expect from each of these activities on your first day at work. Keep in mind that these are general activities and will differ from one organization to another.

Reporting to Work

You must be prepared to make a good impression the first day on the job. There are three basic matters that require your attention before you even arrive at your new job.

1. Dress appropriately.

2. Know where to go and who to contact.

3. Bring any required identification and other documents.

The next section discusses each of these concerns in more detail and contains some checklists to help you prepare for your first day at work. You can get the information you need to complete the checklists by asking the personnel department or your supervisor what you'll need on your first day at work.

Dress Appropriately

It can be very embarrassing to show up for work dressed the wrong way. You'll stand out like a sore thumb and people will remember you for weeks or months because of how you looked that first day. You should ask your supervisor what type of clothing is suitable or required for the job. Think about any special dress situations that may be necessary for your job.

1. What are these and other special clothing requirements employers may have?

_____

_____

_____

_____

Your employer may require you to wear a uniform. If so, find out if it will be issued on your first day or if you are to arrive in uniform on the first day. You will also want to know if you are expected to buy the uniform or if the company provides it.

Certain jobs require special types of safety clothing. Working with chemicals demands a variety of clothing depending on how toxic the chemicals are. Hard hats and steel-toed saftey shoes are required on some jobs to avoid injury. Working near machinery may require you to avoid wearing jewelry or loose clothing that could get caught in mechanical parts.

Be aware of your organization's safety requirements and obey them. The topic of safety clothing and obeying safety regulations will be covered in chapter 3.

Organizations where no special clothing is required still have expectations about the way you dress. When you visit an organization for interviews, notice how the workers dress. After you are hired, ask your supervisor to advise you about what is appropriate to wear on your first day at work.

Dress Checklist

Examine this dress checklist. Pay special attention to the items you may need to wear the first day of your new job.

Uniform

___ Does employer provide uniform?   ___ Where do I pick it up?

___ When do I need it?   ___ How many do I receive?

Safety Clothing

___ Hard hat   ___ Apron

___ Safety goggles   ___ Gloves

___ Hearing protection   ___ Steel-toed boots

___ Safety mask   ___ Other protective clothing

Work Clothes

___ Suits   ___ Skirts/jackets

___ Shirts/blouses   ___ Shoes

___ Pants/slacks   ___ Ties

___ Jeans   ___ Jewelry

___ Dresses

©1992, JIST Works, Inc. • Indianapolis, Indiana

Starting the Day

Talk with your supervisor or personnel department before your first day on the job. Know exactly when you are to arrive, where to go, and who to contact. At some companies, you will report at a different time and location on the first work day than you will on other work days. The questions in the following checklist can help you make sure you know how to report properly for your first day of work.

First Day Checklist

Check off each item as you answer the question.

_____ What time should I arrive? _____

_____ Where should I report? _____

_____ Who should I report to? _____

_____ What documentation should I bring? _____

_____ What special equipment do I need? _____

_____ What will I be expected to do? _____

_____ Where can I store my lunch? _____

Orientation

Many employers will conduct orientation training for new employees on their first day. In some organizations this is the responsibility of the personnel department, while in others it is done by the supervisor. Several important issues may be discussed during orientation including the following subjects.[2]

- **Introduction.** You need to know what the organization does, how it is structured, and who the key people are.
- **Payroll and Personnel Information.** You must complete certain forms for payroll withholdings. You must also prove that you are a U.S. citizen. If you are an immigrant you must prove that you can legally work in this country. Be prepared to provide this information when asked.
- **Policies and Practices Review.** You should be informed about the important policies and practices of your employer. This includes information about vacations, holidays, and other days approved for excused absences.
- **Benefits and Services Review.** You will have a chance to discuss company benefits.
- **Employer Expectation Review.** You should be told what the employer expects. Many of the points reviewed in chapter 1 will be discussed at this time.

The following section explains common benefits and personnel practices among various organizations.[3] Though not all organizations offer the same benefits or follow the same procedures, the explanations here may help you more fully understand the orientation process.

Personnel Information

Most employers need certain documents to verify information about new employees. In most cases, you must provide these documents on or before your first day of work. This information frequently falls into four categories.

1. **Verification of Citizenship/Immigration.** Federal law requires employers to demonstrate that all workers are legally entitled to work in the United States. They must have proof of citizenship or an immigrant work authorization permit for each employee. A copy of your birth certificate is usually enough to document your citizenship.

2. **Social Security Number.** This information is needed to withhold taxes.

3. **Licenses.** Some occupations require a license issued by the state government. If this is the case in your occupation, your employer would need to see the license and keep a copy for company records. The cost and license application is usually the worker's responsibility.

4. **Health Forms.** Your employer may require you to have a physical exam. Most employers pay for the exam and the results go directly to them. However, you may be asked to bring the results when you report in. The President's Commission on Organized Crime has recommended that all companies test employees for drug use.[4] Consequently, your employer may require you to take a drug test. If you are taking prescription medication, you might want to notify the people administering the drug test.

Paperwork

Below are documents that your employer may ask you to bring on your first day of work. Find out which documents you will need and check them off as you collect them — before your first work day. DO IT NOW!

Paperwork Checklist

____ Birth certificate

____ Driver's license

____ Social security identification card

____ Work permit (for workers under 18)

____ Immigrant work authorizaiton (for noncitizens)

____ Medical records (physical exam results)

____ Occupational license (realtor, truck driver, bartender, etc.)

____ Other documents

Applying What You've Learned

Read the following two stories and answer the questions. Both cases describe new employees who could have had a better first day at work. Think about what they might have done to improve their first day on the job.

Case Study 1

Chad arrived at Merlin Controls at 6:45 a.m. ready for his first day at work. He was stopped at the guard's gate from entering the plant because he didn't have an identification badge. Chad explained to the guard that it was his first day at work and gave her the name of his supervisor, Linda. The guard called Linda and asked Chad to wait until she came to escort him into the plant. Linda arrived at the gate 45 minutes later. She apologized to Chad for not coming sooner but she had problems to take care of first. Linda then told Chad since it was his first work day he should report to the personnel office when it opened at 8 a.m. Chad waited in the reception area until the office opened.

1. How would you feel if you were Chad?

   _____

   _____

   _____

2. How could Chad have avoided this problem?

   _____

   _____

   _____

Case Study 2

Felicia was excited about her first day as a claims processor trainee at Adams National Insurance Company and wanted to make a good first impression. She even took an earlier bus to make sure she would arrive on time. When Felicia got to work, she was asked to show her social security card and driver's license for identification purposes, but she did not have them. The personnel officer told her that she could start training that day but would have to bring the documents tomorrow.

1. If you were Felicia, how would this make you feel?

   _____

   _____

   _____

2. How could Felicia have avoided this situation?

   _____

   _____

   _____

Payroll Information and Enrollment

Most employers will ask you to complete payroll information on your first day at work. This section explains what information your employer will require, and why.

Withholding Taxes

There are three forms that typically must be completed by all new employees before they can be added to the payroll. These forms are: 1) a W-4 form for federal withholding taxes, 2) a state tax withholding form, and 3) an I-9 form to check citizenship and legal residence status. Your proof of citizenship or immigrant work authorization form will be used when you complete the I-9 form. The tax withholding forms are used for the following purposes:

- **Federal Income Taxes.** Federal income taxes will automatically be withheld from your paycheck by your employer. The amount of taxes withheld is based on the number of personal allowances that you claim. You will need to complete a W-4 form so that your employer can calculate the correct tax to withhold.

- **State and Local Income Taxes.** Most states and some cities and counties have an income tax. You must complete a withholding form for this tax. Your employer will calculate these local government taxes using the information you provide on the state withholding form to deduct the correct amount from your pay.

- **FICA.** The letters stand for Federal Insurance Contributions Act. This is a social security tax. A set percentage of your paycheck must be withheld by your employer, and your employer contributes a similar amount to your account. This money is used to fund retirement benefits and is credited to your personal account. Your account number is the same as your social security number.

Personal Allowances

The federal government allows you to claim personal allowances for a variety of reasons. An allowance reduces the amount of money on which you pay taxes. You are able to claim an allowance for yourself, your spouse, and any dependents (children, elderly parents, etc.). In addition, special allowances are given if you are the head of a household, have childcare payments in excess of a specific amount each year, and for certain other reasons established by Congress.

Payroll Information

You will probably be told how and when you will be paid when you complete the payroll forms. You should check the following information.

- **Method of Payment.** Many companies now offer employees a choice of being paid by check or direct deposit. A direct deposit places the money in your checking and/or savings account. You will receive a form showing the amount of money your employer deposits in your account. This saves you a trip to the bank to make the deposit yourself. The payroll department can provide you with details if your employer offers this service. You may still choose to receive an actual paycheck you can see and deposit yourself. But be prepared to tell your employer which method you prefer.

- **Schedule of Paydays.** Find out when you will receive your first paycheck. New employees are not always eligible for a paycheck on the first payday after they start work. You should also ask about the regular payday schedule. Some organizations will only distribute paychecks at specific times. If your employer has such a policy and you are not scheduled to work during that time, you'll need to make arrangements to pick up your paycheck.

- **Check Your Withholdings.** You can expect 15 percent or more of your check to be withheld for taxes and other deductions. Check the calculations for withholdings and deductions after you receive your first paycheck. If you don't understand how the calculations were made, talk to the payroll department. Below is a sample deduction form similar to that used by many employers.

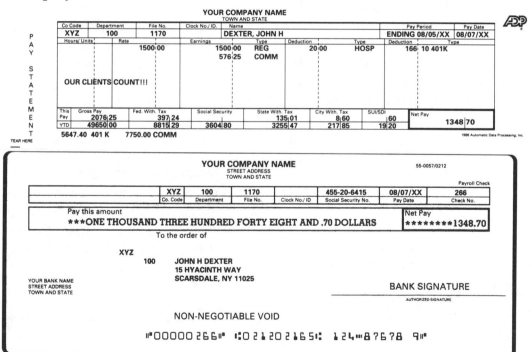

Applying What You've Learned

The following pages contain the Internal Revenue Service Form or W-4. This form is for 1991. The form may change slightly from one year to the next, but this sample will be useful for practice. Assume that you are starting a job today. Complete the form with the correct information for tax withholding.

19**91** Form W-4

**Department of the Treasury
Internal Revenue Service**

Purpose. Complete Form W-4 so that your employer can withhold the correct amount of Federal income tax from your pay.

Exemption From Withholding. Read line 6 of the certificate below to see if you can claim exempt status. *If exempt, complete line 6; but do not complete lines 4 and 5.* No Federal income tax will be withheld from your pay. Your exemption is good for one year only. It expires February 15, 1992.

Basic Instructions. Employees who are not exempt should complete the Personal Allowances Worksheet. Additional worksheets are provided on page 2 for employees to adjust their withholding allowances based on itemized deductions, adjustments to income, or two-earner/two-job situations. Complete all worksheets that apply to your situation. The worksheets will help you figure the number of withholding allowances you are

entitled to claim. However, you may claim fewer allowances than this.

Head of Household. Generally, you may claim head of household filing status on your tax return only if you are unmarried and pay more than 50% of the costs of keeping up a home for yourself and your dependent(s) or other qualifying individuals.

Nonwage Income. If you have a large amount of nonwage income, such as interest or dividends, you should consider making estimated tax payments using Form 1040-ES. Otherwise, you may find that you owe additional tax at the end of the year.

Two-Earner/Two-Jobs. If you have a working spouse or more than one job, figure the total number of allowances you are entitled to claim on all jobs using worksheets from only one Form

W-4. This total should be divided among all jobs. Your withholding will usually be most accurate when all allowances are claimed on the W-4 filed for the highest paying job and zero allowances are claimed for the others.

Advance Earned Income Credit. If you are eligible for this credit, you can receive it added to your paycheck throughout the year. For details, get Form W-5 from your employer.

Check Your Withholding. After your W-4 takes effect, you can use **Pub. 919,** Is My Withholding Correct for 1991?, to see how the dollar amount you are having withheld compares to your estimated total annual tax. Call 1-800-829-3676 to order this publication. Check your local telephone directory for the IRS assistance number if you need further help.

Personal Allowances Worksheet For 1991, the value of your personal exemption(s) is reduced if your income is over $100,000 ($150,000 if married filing jointly, $125,000 if head of household, or $75,000 if married filing separately). Get Pub. 919 for details.

A Enter "1" for **yourself** if no one else can claim you as a dependent . . . . **A** _____

B Enter "1" if:
  { **1.** You are single and have only one job; or
  { **2.** You are married, have only one job, and your spouse does not work; or } . . **B** _____
  { **3.** Your wages from a second job or your spouse's wages (or the total of both) are $1,000 or less. }

C Enter "1" for your **spouse.** But, you may choose to enter "0" if you are married and have either a working spouse or more than one job (this may help you avoid having too little tax withheld) . . . . **C** _____

D Enter number of **dependents** (other than your spouse or yourself) whom you will claim on your tax return . . . . . . **D** _____

E Enter "1" if you will file as **head of household** on your tax return (see conditions under "Head of Household," above) . . **E** _____

F Enter "1" if you have at least $1,500 of **child or dependent care expenses** for which you plan to claim a credit . . . . **F** _____

G Add lines A through F and enter total here . . . . ▶ **G** _____

For accuracy, do all worksheets that apply.
{
• If you plan to **itemize or claim adjustments to income** and want to reduce your withholding, see the Deductions and Adjustments Worksheet on page 2.
• If you are **single** and have **more than one job** and your combined earnings from all jobs exceed $27,000 OR if you are **married** and have a **working spouse or more than one job,** and the combined earnings from all jobs exceed $46,000, see the Two-Earner/Two-Job Worksheet on page 2 if you want to avoid having too little tax withheld.
• If **neither** of the above situations applies, **stop here** and enter the number from line G on line 4 of Form W-4 below.
}

------------------------ **Cut here and give the certificate to your employer. Keep the top portion for your records.** ------------------------

Form **W-4** Department of the Treasury Internal Revenue Service	**Employee's Withholding Allowance Certificate** ▶ **For Privacy Act and Paperwork Reduction Act Notice, see reverse.**	OMB No. 1545-0010 19**91**

1 Type or print your first name and middle initial   Last name | **2** Your social security number

Home address (number and street or rural route)

City or town, state, and ZIP code

3 Marital status
☐ Single ☐ Married
☐ Married, but withhold at higher Single rate.
Note: *If married, but legally separated, or spouse is a nonresident alien, check the Single box.*

4 Total number of allowances you are claiming (from line G above or from the Worksheets on back if they apply) . . . **4**

5 Additional amount, if any, you want deducted from each pay . . . . **5** $

6 I claim exemption from withholding and I certify that I meet **ALL** of the following conditions for exemption:
• Last year I had a right to a refund of **ALL** Federal income tax withheld because I had **NO** tax liability; **AND**
• This year I expect a refund of **ALL** Federal income tax withheld because I expect to have **NO** tax liability; **AND**
• This year if my income exceeds $550 and includes nonwage income, another person cannot claim me as a dependent.

If you meet all of the above conditions, enter the year effective and "EXEMPT" here . . . . . ▶ **6** | 19

7 Are you a full-time student? (**Note:** *Full-time students are not automatically exempt.*) . . . . **7** ☐ Yes ☐ No

Under penalties of perjury, I certify that I am entitled to the number of withholding allowances claimed on this certificate or entitled to claim exempt status.

Employee's signature ▶   Date ▶   , 19

8 Employer's name and address (**Employer:** Complete 8 and 10 **only if sending to IRS**) | **9** Office code (optional) | **10** Employer identification number

Form W-4 (1991)   Page **2**

Deductions and Adjustments Worksheet

Note: *Use this worksheet only if you plan to itemize deductions or claim adjustments to income on your 1991 tax return.*

1   Enter an estimate of your 1991 itemized deductions. These include: qualifying home mortgage interest, charitable contributions, state and local taxes (but not sales taxes), medical expenses in excess of 7.5% of your income, and miscellaneous deductions. (For 1991, you may have to reduce your itemized deductions if your income is over $100,000 ($50,000 if married filing separately). Get Pub. 919 for details.) . . . . . . **1** $ _____

2   Enter:
  $5,700 if married filing jointly or qualifying widow(er)
  $5,000 if head of household
  $3,400 if single
  $2,850 if married filing separately . . . . **2** $ _____

3   **Subtract** line 2 from line 1. If line 2 is greater than line 1, enter zero . . . . **3** $ _____

4   Enter an estimate of your 1991 adjustments to income. These include alimony paid and deductible IRA contributions . . **4** $ _____

5   **Add** lines 3 and 4 and enter the total . . . . **5** $ _____

6   Enter an estimate of your 1991 nonwage income (such as dividends or interest income) . . . . . . **6** $ _____

7   **Subtract** line 6 from line 5. Enter the result, but not less than zero . . . . **7** $ _____

8   **Divide** the amount on line 7 by $2,000 and enter the result here. Drop any fraction . . . . . . **8** _____

9   Enter the number from Personal Allowances Worksheet, line G, on page 1 . . . . **9** _____

10   **Add** lines 8 and 9 and enter the total here. If you plan to use the Two-Earner/Two-Job Worksheet, also enter the total on line 1, below. Otherwise, **stop here** and enter this total on Form W-4, line 4 on page 1 . . . . **10** _____

Two-Earner/Two-Job Worksheet

Note: *Use this worksheet only if the instructions for line G on page 1 direct you here.*

1   Enter the number from line G on page 1 (or from line 10 above if you used the Deductions and Adjustments Worksheet) . **1** _____

2   Find the number in **Table 1** below that applies to the **LOWEST** paying job and enter it here . . . . . **2** _____

3   If line 1 is **GREATER THAN OR EQUAL TO** line 2, subtract line 2 from line 1. Enter the result here (if zero, enter "0") and on Form W-4, line 4, on page 1. **DO NOT** use the rest of this worksheet . . . . **3** _____

Note: *If line 1 is **LESS THAN** line 2, enter "0" on Form W-4, line 4, on page 1. Complete lines 4–9 to calculate the additional dollar withholding necessary to avoid a year-end tax bill.*

4   Enter the number from line 2 of this worksheet . . . . **4** _____

5   Enter the number from line 1 of this worksheet . . . . **5** _____

6   **Subtract** line 5 from line 4 . . . . **6** _____

7   Find the amount in **Table 2** below that applies to the **HIGHEST** paying job and enter it here . . . . . **7** $ _____

8   **Multiply** line 7 by line 6 and enter the result here. This is the additional annual withholding amount needed   **8** $ _____

9   Divide line 8 by the number of pay periods remaining in 1991. (For example, divide by 26 if you are paid every other week and you complete this form in December of 1990.) Enter the result here and on Form W-4, line 5, page 1. This is the additional amount to be withheld from each paycheck . . . . **9** $ _____

Table 1: Two-Earner/Two-Job Worksheet

Married Filing Jointly		All Others	
If wages from **LOWEST** paying job are—	Enter on line 2 above	If wages from **LOWEST** paying job are—	Enter on line 2 above
0 - $4,000	0	0 - $6,000	0
4,001 - 8,000	1	6,001 - 10,000	1
8,001 - 12,000	2	10,001 - 14,000	2
12,001 - 17,000	3	14,001 - 18,000	3
17,001 - 21,000	4	18,001 - 22,000	4
21,001 - 26,000	5	22,001 - 45,000	5
26,001 - 30,000	6	45,001 and over	6
30,001 - 35,000	7		
35,001 - 40,000	8		
40,001 - 55,000	9		
55,001 - 75,000	10		
75,001 and over	11		

Table 2: Two-Earner/Two-Job Worksheet

Married Filing Jointly		All Others	
If wages from **HIGHEST** paying job are—	Enter on line 7 above	If wages from **HIGHEST** paying job are—	Enter on line 7 above
0 - $46,000	$320	0 - $26,000	$320
46,001 - 94,000	600	26,001 - 55,000	600
94,001 and over	670	55,001 and over	670

Privacy Act and Paperwork Reduction Act Notice.—We ask for the information on this form to carry out the Internal Revenue laws of the United States. The Internal Revenue Code requires this information under sections 3402(f)(2)(A) and 6109 and their regulations. Failure to provide a completed form will result in your being treated as a single person who claims no withholding allowances. Routine uses of this information include giving it to the Department of Justice for civil and criminal litigation and to cities, states, and the District of Columbia for use in administering their tax laws.

The time needed to complete this form will vary depending on individual circumstances. The estimated average time is: **Recordkeeping** 46 min., **Learning about the law or the form** 10 min., **Preparing the form** 70 min. If you have comments concerning the accuracy of these time estimates or suggestions for making this form more simple, we would be happy to hear from you. You can write to both the **Internal Revenue Service,** Washington, DC 20224, Attention: IRS Reports Clearance Officer, T:FP; and the **Office of Management and Budget,** Paperwork Reduction Project (1545-0010), Washington, DC 20503. **DO NOT** send the tax form to either of these offices. Instead, give it to your employer.

★ U.S.GPO:1990-0-265-084

Fringe Benefits

Employers can attract workers with employee benefits. Some surveys cited in chapter 1 show that benefits are a major reason people work. This section explains the common "fringe" benefits offered by some employers.

Fringe benefits are often available only to full-time employees. Some employers offer no fringe benefits at all. Your employer may make full payment for some of your fringe benefits, however, most employers now require employees to make partial contributions to help pay for finge benefits. Some employers offer cafeteria plans giving you the choice of which benefits you want. (See box below.) The types of fringe benefits most commonly offered include:

- **Health Insurance.** This insurance will pay doctor and hospital expenses. Most health insurance has a standard deductible amount. The deductible is the amount of medical expense you must pay before the insurance company will pay medical bills. Some health plans cover the cost of prescription drugs and dental work. A variation of health insurance is the Health Maintenance Organization (HMO). HMOs typically cover all medical expenses. An HMO plan is based on the assumption that seeking treatment as soon as symptoms appear prevents major problems later.

- **Disability Insurance.** If you are sick or injured for several weeks or more, disability insurance will pay part or all of your salary. These payments usually begin after you have used all of your paid sick leave.

- **Life Insurance.** This type of insurance is particularly important to someone who has dependents because you can designate a person (beneficiary) to receive a payment from the insurance company should you die. Some employers pay for a life insurance policy equal to one year's salary.

- **Retirement Plans.** Organizations sometimes provide retirement plans for long-time employees.

- **Child Care.** Some companies run child care centers that provide low-cost child care for their employees' children. Certain others might reimburse employees for a portion of their child care costs.

Cafeteria Plans

This is a term used to describe an increasingly popular fringe benefit plan in which an employer provides workers with a wide variety of choices. The employer provides a set amount of money and allows each employee to choose how it will be spent. *The Wall Street Journal* says this type of plan will continue to become more individualized.[5] Benefits will be adjusted as workers move through life stages. For example, a young worker starting a family can receive hospital coverage for pregnancy. Later in life, the same worker may want to put that money into a retirement plan.

Here are two rules of thumb for choosing which fringe benefits to accept:

1. If the employer provides the benefit free of charge, you should definitely sign up for it.

2. If the employer requires you to pay part or all of the benefit cost, only sign up for those you really need.

Paid Time Off

Your employer may offer paid time off as a benefit for one or several of the following circumstances. This will vary greatly from one employer to another.

- **Holiday Pay.** The organization may designate holidays on which you will not be required to work. Many organizations pay their employees for holiday time.

- **Paid Sick Leave.** Employers normally establish a limited number of paid days that you may use for sick days each month or year. If you exceed that limit, you won't be paid for days you can't work due to an illness. There are many different methods of accumulating sick time. Make sure you understand the one your employer uses.

- **Vacation Leave.** This is time off paid for by your employer. As a rule, the amount of vacation time increases with the number of years you work for the organization.

- **Jury Duty Leave.** Some states require an employer to pay an employee for time served on a jury. In other cases, even though under no obligation to pay an employee for this duty, the employer voluntarily pays because they feel it is a community responsibility.

- **Funeral Leave.** This leave is given when a member of your immediate family dies. Various organizations may define "immediate family" differently. Ask about your employer's policy.

- **Military Leave.** Members of the Reserve or National Guard are required to attend active duty training for at least two weeks each year. In a national crisis that period can be extended by Congress. Some employers, though not required, will pay you for the time you are on active military leave or pay the difference in salary.

- **Maternity, Paternity and Adoption Leave.** This is time off for your child's birth or adoption. The law requires that maternity leave be treated as sick leave. Paternity and adoption leave may be offered at the discretion of the employer.

Required Benefits

Some employee benefits are required by federal and state laws. These are discussed below.

- **FICA (Federal Insurance Contributions Act).** The employer must match your contribution to the social security fund. This fund will pay benefits to your children who are under age 21 should you die. The fund will also pay you and your dependents if you are disabled for more than 12 months. It will also pay you a pension when you reach retirement age.

- **Unemployment Insurance.** Your employer must contribute to an unemployment insurance fund administered by your state. If you are laid off or dismissed from your job, you may file a claim with your state employment agency. Eligibility requirements vary from state to state. The reasons for unemployment are also taken into consideration. Eligibility is determined by the state employment office. Unemployment benefit amounts are also established by each state. Weekly benefits are paid for 26 weeks or until you find suitable employment, whichever comes first.

- **Worker's Compensation Insurance.** Most states require employers to carry this insurance. This insurance pays for injuries that occur on the job. In addition, you will receive partial payment for time off the job caused by a work-related injury.

Voluntary Deductions

In addition to fringe benefit deductions, your employer can deduct other withholdings from your paycheck with your approval. Some deductions, such as federal and state taxes, are required. Others, like those listed below, are voluntary.

- **Child Support.** You may want to have monthly child support payments automatically deducted from your paycheck. Check with your lawyer or court representative to find out how this is done.

- **Savings Plan.** You may have a portion of your pay sent directly to your bank or credit union account. Use it to make automatic loan payments, add to savings, or some other use.

- **Charity Donations.** Make deductions to contribute to a charity. This arrangement is most often available for United Way organizations.

- **Union Dues.** Most unions make arrangements with an employer to withhold dues directly from your paycheck. In some areas, unions have an agreement with the employer requiring them to withhold dues even if you are not a union member. In such cases you have **no choice** concerning this deduction.

- **Stock Options.** You may be able to have deductions withheld for purchase of company stock. Your employer may require you to be employed by the organization for several years before you are eligible for this benefit.

Employee Services

Employers can provide many different services for their employees. Many employers feel that the more they do for their employees, the more the empoyees will do for them.

- **Educational Assistance Plans.** Employers will often reimburse college or technical school tuition for those employees who are working toward a degree or taking other work-related courses.
- **Employee Assistance Programs.** Employees may receive counseling for personal or work-related problems. This may include treatment for various problems such as drug abuse or alcoholism.
- **Credit Unions.** Credit unions are established in some organizations to provide financial services for employees. Credit unions usually provide these services at a lower cost than banks or savings and loan institutions.
- **Other.** These services may include legal assistance, health services, food service, financial planning, housing and moving expenses, transportation, purchase discounts and recreational services.

Selecting Benefits and Deductions

Assume that you have just started working today. Place a check mark beside those items that you want as fringe benefits or deductions. Assume that the employer would only pay a portion of the following benefits. Write your reasons for selecting or not selecting each item.

____ **Health Insurance**

_____

_____

____ **Dental Insurance**

_____

_____

____ **Prescription Drugs**

_____

_____

____ **Life Insurance**

_____

_____

____ **Disability Insurance**

_____

_____

___ **Retirement Program**

_____

_____

___ **Child Care**

_____

_____

___ **Union Dues**

_____

_____

___ **Savings Plan**

_____

_____

___ **Charity Donation**

_____

_____

___ **Stock Options**

_____

_____

Other Employer-Provided Benefits

Check the following paid time off and employee assistance benefits that are provided by your employer. If you aren't currently employed, check those benefits that you feel are important for an employer to provide.

___ Holiday Leave ___ Paternity Leave

___ Vacation Leave ___ Maternity Leave

___ Jury Duty Leave ___ Educational Assistance

___ Sick Leave ___ Employee Assistance Plan

___ Funeral Leave Credit Unions

___ Military Leave ___ Other (Specify)

1. Why do you feel the benefits you checked are important?

_____

_____

_____

_____

Applying What You've Learned

Now, imagine that you are the people described in the following cases. Answer the questions based on the description of each individual.

Case Study 1

Steve and his wife have a 7-year-old daughter and 3-year-old son. He is a carpenter for a construction firm and is working on a construction technology degree at a local community college. During the past year, the children have been sick several times. Steve and his wife just purchased a new home.

1. List six employee benefits or services that you feel Steve needs.

   _____   _____

   _____   _____

   _____   _____

2. Tell why each benefit is important to Steve.

   _____

   _____

   _____

   _____

   _____

   _____

Case Study 2

Pilar is the branch manager of a local bank. She is divorced and the parent of a 4-year-old daughter. Pilar is active in the Naval Reserve. During the past year she has been mildly depressed about her divorce and has been drinking more than she would like.

1. What benefits do you think would be the most helpful for Pilar?

   _____   _____

   _____   _____

   _____   _____

2. Explain why you think these benefits are important.

   _____

   _____

   _____

   _____

   _____

Introduction to the Job

After orientation, your supervisor will probably take you around the job site or work area. He or she should provide you with the following information, but be prepared to ask about these things anyway.

Work Instructions

It is important that you understand how to do your job. Your supervisor should show and tell you how to do the tasks that make up the job. Here are a few guidelines to follow during this time.

- **Don't be nervous.** You won't be expected to learn everything at once.
- **Relax!** You aren't expected to do everything right the first time.
- **Listen.** Listen carefully and watch closely as the supervisor demonstrates a task.
- **Ask questions.** Be sure to ask questions when you don't understand something you've been told or shown.
- **Learn what is expected.** Make sure you know exactly what the supervisor expects from you.

Supplies and Equipment

You need to know how to obtain the supplies and equipment necessary to do your job properly. The supervisor should give you this information. Some things you might need to know are:

- Supply area location.
- Supply and equipment check-out procedure. You may need to fill out forms requiring your supervisor's approval.
- Person in charge of supply distribution. This person is important. You must know who they are and how to contact them.

Telephone System

All business relies on communication. Even though your job may not involve using the telephone, you must know how to make and answer phone calls. You'll need to know the following information:

- **How to Use the Phone System.** Modern office phones are complex. Ask to be shown how to use the most common features needed to do your job.
- **Telephone Policy.** What are the phone procedures? Who answers your phone if you're away from your desk? What should you say when you answer the phone? Can you make and receive personal phone calls? When you ask this last question, make sure your supervisor understands you mean short, important calls.

Breaks

There are several different types of breaks that you might take throughout the work day. Below are the most common reasons people take work breaks. Many organizations prohibit smoking on the job or restrict it to a smoking room. If you intend to smoke during your break you need to know where it is allowed.

- **Rest Room Break.** You must know where they are located. In some jobs it is necessary to find a replacement to do your job before taking such a break.

- **Rest Break.** Employers often provide a 15 minute break in the first and second half of the work day if you work a full eight hours. Find out when you can take a break and if there is a break room.

- **Meal Break.** You will probably be allowed a meal break around the middle of your work period if you work a full eight hours. Make sure you know when to take a meal break and how much time is allowed.

Some organizations have in-house cafeterias. Others provide a break room where you may eat a sack lunch. Find out if your employer provides a kitchen with a refrigerator and/or microwave oven for employee use.

Your supervisor should explain what you need to know about work tasks, supplies, telephone systems, and breaks. If your supervisor forgets to tell you anything, don't be afraid to ask! This is an important basic rule during the first few days on the job.

Off to a Good Start

After your supervisor shows you around, you'll be on your own. It is important to realize that you will start a new job the same way everyone else does. You won't know very much about the job. You probably won't know anyone there either. You may wonder if you can do the job and if you'll like it there. Here are some suggestions that will help you adjust to the job during the first few weeks.

Tips for Adjustment to the New Job

- **Be Positive.** Expect good things to happen. Starting a new job gives you the opportunity to prove yourself to your supervisor and co-workers.

- **Ask for Help.** Your supervisor and co-workers will expect you to ask questions. They will be willing to help when you ask. Listen carefully so you don't have to ask the same question more than once.

- **Don't Be a Know-It-All.** You are new on the job. No matter how much you know and how skilled you are, you don't know everything about this particular job. Take the first few weeks to learn. You will gain the respect of your co-workers and supervisor by demonstrating your ability to do your job well. Then you can begin making suggestions to improve the way things are done.

- **Have a Good Sense of Humor.** New workers may be tested by other workers. Some may want to see how you respond to teasing and practical jokes. You could consider this an initiation. Try your best to accept good-natured teasing. If things get out of hand and you feel unfairly treated or abused, talk with your supervisor about the situation.

- **Find a Buddy.** Look for someone who seems to know the job well and ask them to help you if you need it. Sometimes your supervisor will assign someone to help you the first few days on the job. Listen to and respect this person. They know the job better than you do.

- **Follow Instructions.** Your supervisor is the most important person in your work life. That person will assign your work, decide whether you continue on the job, get promoted and receive pay increases. Follow instructions, be helpful, and do the best possible job. This is what most supervisors want and reward.

- **Read Company Policies.** Companies often provide employees with printed materials explaining their policies and procedures. Read this carefully. Ignorance will not be considered a reason for doing something wrong or not knowing what to do.

The first few days on the job are important. They often determine the way you will permanently feel about the job. Following the suggestions in this chapter can help you make the first few days on your job a more positive experience.

Applying What You've Learned

The following cases present problems that often occur within the first few days on the job. Read them and respond to the questions.

Case Study 1

Craig arrived at his new job as a stock clerk today. His supervisor, Sharon, introduced him to the other workers. She then showed him what he would do for the day. This included taking him around the store and explaining how the shelves should be stocked, when to stock the products and where to get new items to put on the shelves, and how to price the items. Sharon then left Craig on his own. Everything went fine until he found some products he wasn't sure how to price. Craig didn't want to appear stupid, so he went ahead and marked the prices the best way he could.

1. What would you have done if you were Craig?

   _____

   _____

2. What problems do you think Craig might have caused?

   _____

   _____

Case Study 2

Vicky is a new secretary for a law firm. Her supervisor gave her a tour of the office, introduced her to other workers and told her what tasks she would be doing. She then told Vicky if she had questions to contact her in her office. Assume this is all Vicky had been told. List five questions you would ask if you were Vicky.

1. _____

2. _____

3. _____

4. _____

5. _____

Summary

Preparation is the key to creating that positive first impression your first day on a new job. The information, exercises, and checklists in this chapter will give you a good idea of what to expect. You can't always prepare for every situation, but the more issues you're aware of and the more questions you have answered before you start work will help you survive those first-day-on-the-job blues.

Chapter Two Endnotes

1. Beverly Gerber, "Annual Industry Report on Training," *Training Magazine*, October 1989.

2. Ronald Smith, "Employee Orientation: Steps to Success," *Personnel Journal*, December 1984, 46-48.

3. Robert L. Mathis, and John H. Jackson, *Personnel: Human Resource Management*, (West Publishing Co., St. Paul, Minn., 1983).

4. Ian Miners and Nick Nykodym, "Put Drug Detection to the Test," *Personnel Journal*, August 1987, 91-97.

5. "More Benefits Bend with Worker's Needs," *Wall Street Journal*, 9 January 1990, B1.

Chapter Three

Making a Good Impression

I Haven't a Thing to Wear

Our impressions affect the way we treat people. This is a natural human reaction. Therefore, it shouldn't surprise you that the impressions other people have about you will affect the way they treat you. People form impressions based on looks and actions. Your physical appearance often determines what kind of first impression you will make.

It is important that you look as good as possible. This will help you make a positive impression on other people. "Wait a minute," you say, "I'm not *that* good looking. Do you expect me to get plastic surgery?" No, this chapter isn't about how to change your body. It's about how to take advantage of your physical characteristics to look the best you can. John Molloy wrote a book called *Dress For Success*.[1] He advises professionals how to dress for managerial and executive positions. Molloy's research on the importance of dress in the workplace indicates your dress has a major impact on the impressions others form of you.

Hygiene (personal body care) can also influence what impression you make on people. Messy hair, bad breath and body odor make a poor impression. People will avoid you. Co-workers will not want to work in the same area as you. This chapter will help you determine proper ways to dress for your job as well as the basics of good hygiene.

One team of experts expresses the result of a poor physical appearance this way: "In certain situations, dress can even be as important to job success as worker skills. Superiors and subordinates make certain decisions based solely on appearance. So it is to the worker's advantage to dress appropriately."[2] In other words, people assume that you will care for your job in the same way you care for yourself.

Wearing the Right Clothes

It is important to remember that clothes influence the way people perceive you. These perceptions will affect how well you are accepted by your supervisor and co-workers.[3] Below are some general guidelines about what to wear on the job.

- **Dress Codes.** The best way to know how to dress is to ask. Your supervisor and co-workers know about official and unofficial dress codes for your job. Official dress codes must be fair. However, unofficial dress codes can affect work assignments, pay raises, and promotions.

- **Appropriate Dress.** You may have some very nice clothes that make you look attractive. However, they may not be appropriate for the workplace. Clothes you would wear for a night on the town probably aren't appropriate for the workplace. Neither are tight fitting clothes, low-cut dresses, unbuttoned shirts, short skirts, and flashy colored outfits.

- **Neat Dress.** Make sure the clothes you wear are neat and clean. Press them if necessary. Your clothes should be in good shape, with no rips or tears. Shoes should be clean and in good condition, and polished if necessary.

- **Uniforms.** Some businesses require their employees to wear uniforms at work. Here are some things you need to consider about uniforms.

  —Who is responsible to keep uniforms clean and pressed? (Some employers have a cleaning service.)

  —How many uniforms will you need?

  —Who is responsible for accidental damage to the uniform? (Something other than normal wear and tear.)

  —How should the uniform be worn? (Are certain types of shoes or blouses, etc. to be worn with it?)

- **Safety Clothing.** Some jobs present possible safety hazards. In such occupations, you may be required to wear certain clothing. Here are some common safety considerations.

  —Loose clothing or dangling jewelry may get caught and pull you into moving equipment. Avoid wearing such items if you work around moving equipment.

  —Hard leather shoes are a must on a job if something heavy could drop on your feet. Sometimes you may be required to wear steel-toed shoes for protection.

  —Jeans will help protect you from scratches and cuts that may occur on some jobs.

Special Safety Equipment

Certain jobs require certain protective dress considerations. Find out what safety equipment is required on the job, and wear it. Safety equipment tends to be slightly uncomfortable, but failure to wear the equipment can result in losing your job. Your employer is responsible for your safety and should not tolerate safety infractions. Below is a list of common safety equipment and reasons each article is worn.

- **Safety Glasses.** Safety glasses are required in jobs where small particles could strike or lodge in your eyes. Workers drilling on metal parts would find it necessary to wear safety glasses.

- **Ear Protectors.** Exposure to continuous or loud noise can cause hearing problems. You are required to wear ear protectors when you work in such jobs. Ground personnel who work around jet airplanes wear ear protectors to protect their hearing.

- **Hard Hats.** If you work where falling objects are a risk, you are required to wear a hard hat. This may not protect you from all injuries, but it can reduce the seriousness of an injury. Most construction workers are usually required to wear hard hats.

- **Masks.** Exposure to fumes from dangerous chemicals is unavoidable in some jobs. Different types of masks protect workers from a variety of toxic fumes. Failure to wear a mask when required could result in serious injury or death. A painter in a body and trim shop would probably wear a mask.

- **Gloves.** Frostbite, blisters or rope burns are hazards in some jobs. A person stacking hay bales or working in the frozen food section of a grocery store would probably wear gloves.

- **Protective Clothing.** Those who work with or near hazardous material must often wear protective clothing. This includes gloves, aprons, coveralls, boots, or an entire protective suit. If you work with hazardous materials, your employer must provide the protective clothing you need and teach you how to protect yourself from harm.

Applying What You've Learned

Go through the following exercises and check how you think each person should dress for the job described.

Exercise 1

Jill is an accountant for a life insurance company. Check the items you think she should wear to work.

____Blouse	____Shirt
____Boots	____Shorts
____Business Suit	____Skirt
____Casual Shoes	____Slacks
____Dress	____Socks
____Dress shirt	____Sweater
____Jacket	____T-shirt
____Jeans	____Tie
____Jewelry	____Vest
____Leather shoes	____Tennis shoes
____Nylons	____ Other _____
____Pants	____ Other _____

1. Why did you select these items?

_____

_____

_____

Exercise 2

Yvonne is a delivery person for a pizza restaurant. Check the items you think she should wear to work.

____Blouse	____Shirt
____Boots	____Shorts
____Business Suit	____Skirt
____Casual Shoes	____Slacks
____Dress	____Socks
____Dress shirt	____Sweater
____Jacket	____T-shirt
____Jeans	____Tie
____Jewelry	____Vest
____Leather shoes	____Tennis shoes
____Nylons	____ Other _____
____Pants	____ Other _____

1. Why did you select these items?

_____

_____

_____

Exercise 3

Roger works as a counter person in a dry cleaners. Check the items you think he should wear to work.

___ Blouse   ___ Shirt

___ Boots   ___ Shorts

___ Business Suit   ___ Skirt

___ Casual Shoes   ___ Slacks

___ Dress   ___ Socks

___ Dress shirt   ___ Sweater

___ Jacket   ___ T-shirt

___ Jeans   ___ Tie

___ Jewelry   ___ Vest

___ Leather shoes   ___ Tennis shoes

___ Nylons   ___ Other _____

___ Pants   ___ Other _____

1. Why did you select these items?

_____

_____

_____

Exercise 4

Calvin is a production worker in an automotive parts factory. Check the items you think he should wear to work.

___ Blouse   ___ Nylons

     Boots   Pants

___ Business Suit   ___ Shirt

___ Casual Shoes   ___ Shorts

___ Dress   ___ Skirt

___ Dress shirt   ___ Slacks

___ Jacket   ___ Socks

___ Jeans   ___ Sweater

___ Jewelry   ___ T-shirt

___ Leather shoes   ___ Tie

____Vest   ____ Other _____

____Tennis shoes   ____ Other _____

1. Why did you select these items?

_____

_____

_____

Exercise 5

Shellie is a telephone repair person. Check the items you think she should wear to work.

____Blouse   ____Shirt

____Boots   ____Shorts

____Business Suit   ____Skirt

____Casual Shoes   ____Slacks

____Dress   ____Socks

____Dress shirt   ____Sweater

____Jacket   ____T-shirt

____Jeans   ____Tie

____Jewelry   ____Vest

____Leather shoes   ____Tennis shoes

____Nylons   ____ Other _____

____Pants   ____ Other _____

1. Why did you select these items?

_____

_____

_____

Exercise 6

Stan is a lab assistant at a hospital. Check the items you think he should wear to work.

____Blouse   ____Nylons

____Boots   ____Pants

____Business Suit   ____Shirt

____Casual Shoes   ____Shorts

____Dress   ____Skirt

____Dress shirt   ____Slacks

____Jacket   ____Socks

____Jeans   ____Sweater

____Jewelry   ____T-shirt

____Leather shoes   ____Tie

___ Vest   ___ Other _____

___ Tennis shoes   ___ Other _____

1. Why did you select these items?

   _____

   _____

   _____

Postive Grooming

Grooming habits that your friends accept or seemed adequate while you were in school may cause you problems at work. Imagine a typical morning as you prepare for work or school.

1. List the hygiene and grooming activities you practice.

   _____

   _____

   _____

2. What other kinds of grooming do you practice on a periodic basis? How often?

   _____

   _____

   _____

3. How would you rate your appearance after going through the activities listed above?

   ___ **I look perfect.** Anyone would like to be with me.

   ___ **I look good.** My friends, co-workers, and supervisor would like to be with me.

   ___ **I look fine.** At least my friends and family would like to be with me.

   ___ **I could look better.** I like to be by myself.

   ___ **I don't look very good.** Even my dog wouldn't like to be with me.

4. How can you improve your grooming so your appearance would be acceptable to anyone? Be honest.

   _____

   _____

   _____

Good Grooming Habits

Below is a checklist of grooming activities that you should practice on a regular basis. Place a plus (+) next to those that you do regularly and a minus (-) next to those you could improve.

_____**Showering or Bathing**. You need to regularly shower or bathe. It is not pleasant to work with someone who has body odor.

_____**Using Deodorant.** Use some type of antiperspirant, deodorant or body powder daily. This helps control body odor that occurs from sweating.

_____**Brushing Your Teeth.** Brush your teeth at least once a day and when possible after each meal. Bad breath will make people want to avoid you.

_____**Gargling with Mouthwash.** It is debatable how much mouthwash helps control bad breath. However, if you have a problem with bad breath, use mouthwash once or twice a day.

_____**Shaving.** Facial hair can be a distraction in the work setting. If facial hair causes workers to concentrate on you rather than the job, it becomes a distraction, and supervisors have a right to deal with such issues in the workplace.[4] In many occupations, this means shaving regularly, typically whenever stubble appears. While a moustache has become acceptable in most jobs, a beard still causes suspicion in many organizations. If you want to wear a beard and/or moustache and find that it is accepted, remember to groom your moustache and beard on a daily basis and keep them neatly trimmed.

_____**Shampooing.** Shampoo your hair every one to three days. The oiliness of your hair will determine how often.

_____**Styling Hair.** Your hair will always look much better when you keep it trimmed and take time to style it. Talk with a hair stylist about keeping your hair looking good every day. At the least, comb your hair several times a day. Wear hair styles appropriate for the workplace and your lifestyle.

_____**Trimming Hair.** Keep your hair trimmed on a regular basis. Extremely long hair on either sex may be considered unconventional in some organizations. Long hair worn down may be considered a safety problem in certain jobs and must be pinned up. Long hair worn loose is also a hygienic consideration in jobs such as food preparation.

_____**Trimming Fingernails.** Fingernails should be kept clean and neatly trimmed. Women who wear fingernail polish should stick with conservative colors for work.

_____**Using Makeup**. Makeup can help you look your best, but not when it's applied wrong. Natural colors that compliment your skin tone are appropriate. Bold colors such as hot pink and purple are rarely appropriate in the workplace. If you're not sure how to correctly apply makeup to enhance your looks, ask the consultant at a cosmetic counter.

> ### A Word About Cologne: Moderation
>
> Colognes and perfumes can smell pleasant, but too much of either is offensive to many people.[5] Overpowering odor is not appropriate in the workplace no matter what the source. Some people have allergies to colognes and perfumes. You should be considerate of co-workers and not aggravate this condition. Masking body odor is not the purpose of colognes and perfumes. If you have excessive body odor follow the grooming tips above.

Special Hygiene Concerns

In some jobs your own health, as well as that of customers or patients, depends upon your good hygienic practices. For example, health care organizations and food preparation facilities are required by law to enforce certain sanitary practices. Below is a list of the most commonly required hygienic practices.

- **Hair Nets.** Hair nets are sometimes required for jobs in food service or food preparation.
- **Washing Hands.** You need to wash your hands with soap and water after using the rest room. This helps protect you from disease or from spreading germs. This is particularly important in jobs where you prepare or serve food. Regulations require workers in health occupations to wash their hands each time they work with a patient.
- **Gloves.** Gloves will help control exposure to germs in food preparation and health occupations.
- **Aprons.** Aprons may be required in food preparation jobs to prevent germs, dirt or other foreign particles on your clothes from getting into the food.

This list provides just a few examples of hygienic practices on the job. Additional precautions are taken in many occupations. You should become familiar with the hygiene practices, if any, required for your job. In some cases, such as food preparation jobs, there will be state and local laws that govern hygiene.

Special Personal Considerations

There are three specific issues regarding appearance that justify special attention. These issues are physical condition, weight, and acne. Let's examine these one at a time.

1. **Physical Condition.** This applies to everyone. You need to exercise regularly to be in good physical condition. Exercise improves your stamina and allows you to work harder and longer. This pays off when you are rewarded with higher pay and/or promotions because of your productivity. Being in good shape applies equally to workers in either physically or mentally demanding jobs.

2. **Weight.** People who are overweight may encounter some difficulty in the way other people react to them. Call it discrimination. Many in our society think overweight people are less attractive. Some even perceive overweight people as being lazy—quite an obstacle for the hopeful employee to overcome. If you are overweight you should do as much as possible to improve your appearance. This may mean going on a diet and exercising more. Do your best to overcome any weight problem.

3. **Acne.** Many people have a problem with acne. Occasional skin breakouts are not usually as ugly or terrible as people who suffer from them think they are. If you have a serious problem with acne, consult a dermatologist. A better diet and skin care and medication may help improve this condition.

Problems in any of these areas may cause people to think less of themselves. While physical attractiveness may be a factor in getting ahead at work, a positive self-image and good mental attitude are more important. If you have a problem with your appearance, do your best to look as good as you can. Then concentrate on other things. No one can do more than their best.

Mannerisms

Mannerisms can have as powerful an influence on people as appearance. Look at other people and determine what mannerisms they exhibit that negatively affect the way you feel about them. Examine yourself for any such behavior. Ask friends and family to tell you if they observe undesirable traits in your conduct. (Family will be especially willing to do this.) Listed below are some common problems.

- **Gum Chewing.** It is difficult to speak clearly when chewing gum. In addition to making speech difficult to understand, it distorts facial expressions.

- **Slang.** Many people will not understand slang or will think the user is ignorant or uneducated. You should use a commonly understood vocabulary. The curser is even worse, appearing not only ignorant, but also rude and uncouth.

- **Picking and Pulling.** Sometimes people unconsciously develop a habit of picking at a certain part of their body like ears, nose, hair, chin, or fingers. It can be very distracting or even disgusting to other people.

Applying What You've Learned

Dressing correctly for your job is one of the most important things that you can do to keep your job. The first impression you make each day will greatly affect the way others treat you. Following are case studies of two workers. Answer the questions about dress and hygiene.

Case Study 1

Sasha works with you in a large office. She started work as a secretary about four weeks ago. Today she came into the office dressed in a short skirt that is quite revealing when she sits down. She has on so much perfume that you can smell it 20 feet away. Her nails are very long and decorated. Her eyes are highlighted in purple to match her dress color. Her lipstick is also purple. She is wearing spiked heels and black mesh nylons.

1. What is your first reaction when you see Sasha?

   _____

   _____

2. Your supervisor just told you that Sasha will be helping you complete a proposal for a potential client. Do you think Sasha will be a good worker? Explain the reason for your answer.

   _____

   _____

Case Study 2

Rolf is a maintenance worker at large hospital. He is required to wear a uniform to work. His hair is not very well trimmed. Some employees avoid him, saying that he doesn't smell very good. Once in a while he has stubble on his face.

1. List what you think Rolf should do to properly groom himself for this job.

   _____

   _____

2. Are there any on-the-job hygienic habits that Rolf should keep in mind?

   _____

   _____

Summary

Proper dress and good hygiene are crucial for two important reasons. First, they affect your appearance, and your appearance has an effect on supervisors, co-workers, and customers — either good or bad. Appropriate dress and grooming guidelines should always be followed. Your supervisor and co-workers should provide a good example in these matters. Secondly, proper dress and hygiene may be important to your health and safety. Wearing clothes that can protect you from injury or disease is important. Find out what the safety and health requirements are for your job and follow them closely. Rules about safety and health equipment are for your own good.

Chapter Three Endnotes

1. John T.Malloy, *Dress For Success*, (Warner Books, New York, 1975).

2. Shane R. Premeaux and R. Wayne Mondy, "People Problems: Dress Distractions," *Management Solutions*, January 1987, 35-37.

3. Kenneth Oldfield and Nancy Ayers, "Avoid the New Job Blues," *Personnel Journal*, August 1986, 49-56.

4. Premeaux op. cit., 35-37.

5. Leah Rosch, "The Professional Image Report," *Working Woman*, October 1988, 109.

Chapter Four
Punctuality and Attendance

Organizations Need
Dependable People

An organization can't operate without dependable workers. A supervisor must be able to rely on employees coming to work every day on time. When a worker is late or absent, it causes many problems. In fact, employers list absenteeism as one of the major reasons for firing employees.[1]

Problems Caused by Absenteeism and Tardiness

The following exercise shows what can happen when employees are unreliable. Put yourself in George's place. He supervises the morning shift in a fast food restaurant. The phone rings at 6 a.m. It's Lee, who has worked in the restaurant for one month. "George, this is Lee. My car won't start so I won't be at work today." The breakfast crowd has started to arrive in the dining area. Several cars have pulled in to the drive up window.

1. What problems did Lee create by not coming to work?

   _____

   _____

   _____

2. How does Lee's absence affect other workers at the restaurant?

   _____

   _____

   _____

3. How many times do you think George should allow Lee to be absent from work before taking some kind of action?

   _____

   _____

   _____

There are several problems you may have listed that were caused by Lee's absence. Below are some of the problems caused by workers who arrive late or do not come to work. You may have listed some of them in the previous exercise.

- **Problems for the Employer.** Employee absence can cost an organization money in two ways.

  1. **Reduced Productivity.** Less workers means the organization produces fewer goods or cannot serve as many customers. In some instances the amount of goods and services remains the same but the quality suffers. This costs the organization money.

  2. **Customer Dissatisfaction.** Customers won't be served as well as they should be. For instance, if a worker in a production-related job is absent, a customer's shipment may not be made on time because there wasn't enough help. This also costs the organization money.

> ## Customer Satisfaction
>
> Americans know the importance of satisfying customers. Business leaders like Tom Peters, a leading management expert, emphasize the need for good customer service to be competitive in today's business world.[2] Think about it. Do you go to stores where the clerks treat you poorly? Do you return to a restaurant that takes a long time to bring your food? Of course not. That is why it is important for a business to provide high quality customer service. They want customers to come back and continue to make purchases. Good customer service is difficult for a business to provide without dependable workers.

- **Problems for Supervisors.** Worker absence means supervisors must rearrange work schedules and plans. Another worker may have to fill in. Problems created by one absence or tardiness usually continue throughout the day. Supervisors usually pick up the slack which could make them angry. How the supervisor reacts depends largely on the reason and frequency of the absence.

- **Problems for Co-workers.** Everyone must work harder when another worker is absent. Consequently, one absence also creates problems for co-workers. A person who had the day off may be called to come into work. Someone who just finished a shift may be asked to stay and work a double shift. They too may be angry at the absent employee.

- **Problems for the Employee.** Being absent or tardy will often result in "docked" pay. This means no pay for the time off work. The organization's policy about days off will affect how much the paycheck is cut. As previously stated, relationships with supervisors and co-workers are negatively affected by absenteeism and tardiness. Repeated incidents could result in getting fired.

What's Your Excuse?

There are many reasons workers are absent or tardy. Sometimes being absent or late is unavoidable. Read the following list. Place a check mark in the "A" column if that reason causes you to be absent frequently. Check "L" if it makes you late and "B" if that reason causes you to be both late and absent on different occasions. If you aren't currently employed, check those reasons you were late or absent from a former job or school.

Reason	Absent	Late	Both
Overslept			
Missed the bus			
Personal illness			
Alarm didn't ring			
Children were sick			
Car didn't start			
Couldn't find a babysitter			
Someone borrowed the car			
Wanted to sleep in			
Traffic was bad			
Didn't feel like going			
Family problems			
Wanted to do other things			
Weather was bad			
Forgot the work schedule			
No clean clothes			
Hangover			
Took a trip instead			
Needed a day off			

As you look over this list, be aware of what you need to do to reduce your personal absence and tardiness from work. The next section reviews ways that you can avoid the problems listed in the exercise above.

How Lifestyle Affects Your Work

A lifestyle is made up of the habits and activities that you develop for day-to-day living. It includes what you eat, when and how long you sleep, and other daily activities. Physicians and other scientists know that your lifestyle can affect the amount of stress in your daily life. Dr. Peter Hanson, physician and lecturer on stress, points out that stress affects your health and emotions.[3] Many of the reasons people miss work are directly related to their lifestyle. Here are some ways you can mold your lifestyle to increase your success at work.

- **Get A Good Night's Sleep.** Most people need 6 to 8 hours of sleep each night. Your body rests better when you sleep on a regular schedule. Many young people make the mistake of going to parties or other social activities on work nights. This can result in less sleep. Then they often skip work the next morning or wake up late for work. Not having enough sleep will lower your energy level on the job. You will not work as efficiently or enthusiastically without sufficient sleep.

- **Eat Well.** Eat well-balanced meals on a regular schedule and avoid too much junk food. Consume plenty of fruits and vegetables. You are less likely to be ill when you have good eating habits.

- **Exercise Regularly.** The majority of jobs in the U.S. are service- and information-related jobs and don't require much exercise. Regular exercise keeps a person in top physical and mental condition and aids the release of job-related stress.

- **Avoid Smoking.** A Robert Half International survey reports that one in four employers will reject a smoker who is competing for a job against an equally qualified non-smoker.[4] There is plenty of medical evidence to prove smoking is hazardous to both smokers and non-smokers. Many organizations offer incentives and help for employees who want to stop smoking.

- **Avoid Excessive Alcohol Consumption.** Alcohol can cause health problems. The more alcohol you drink, the more you may damage your body. Drinking to excess will reduce your performance on the job the next day. Drinking during or right before work is often cause for dismissal.

- **Avoid Drugs.** Illegal drugs are harmful to the body and mind. You should not take any drugs unless specifically prescribed for you by a physician. Policies about illegal drug use vary among organizations. If you test positive for certain drugs, some organizations give you a choice of entering a rehabilitation program or being fired. Other employers will simply fire you outright.

- **Keep Good Company.** Your relationships can affect your work. For instance, if your friends don't work, they may want you to adapt to their schedule which may make you too tired for work the next day. If a conflict like this occurs you need to establish a priority for work and social activities. Avoid people who may get you into trouble with the law. Employers do not appreciate workers who miss work because they are in jail. In fact, you could get fired for missing work for that reason if your employer finds out. Many people make friends and socialize with other employed people to avoid such problems.

- **Socializing with Co-workers.** Socializing means participating in activities with other people. We all need time to socialize with friends and acquaintances. Our co-workers often become our best friends because we spend so much time with them. Relationships with co-workers can be very positive or quickly turn sour. Here are guidelines to help you avoid problems in work relationships.

—**Avoid romances with co-workers.** They can make relationships with other co-workers awkward and often create unpleasant situations when the romance ends.

—**Don't limit friendships to just co-workers.** One thing that can happen when you socialize with co-workers is that you spend a lot of time talking about work. You need to mentally get away from your job to reduce stress. This means not talking or even thinking about the job.

—**Don't let friendships with co-workers interfere with your work performance.** Don't do someone else's work to cover for their inability or laziness. Don't side with a friend against another worker or supervisor. Try to be neutral in work relationships.

Your Lifestyle and Stress

A moderate lifestyle will serve you well throughout your life. Moderation is avoiding excess. Rate your lifestyle using the following checklist. Check each statement that is true for you. Then, score your answers to see how you measure up to good lifestyle habits that can make you a better worker.

____I do something really fun on a regular basis.

____I rarely drink to excess.

____I exercise regularly.

____I have friends I can rely on.

____I gain strength from my religious beliefs.

____I avoid eating lots of junk food.

____I don't smoke.

____I average 6 to 8 hours of sleep on work nights.

____I do not use illegal drugs.

____I eat at least one well-balanced meal daily.

Count the number of statements you checked. Score yourself using the following guidelines:

8 or More: Reflects a positive lifestyle, effective on the job. **6 to 7:** Reflects moderate lifestyle, will assist you on the job. **5 or Less:** Reflects a vulnerable lifestyle, you may find your lifestyle creates some job problems.

Planning to Get to Work

Managing your life through good planning will help you avoid missing work. There are five major steps you can take to ensure a good work attendance record. Often people who are frequently absent from work have not considered these five steps.

1. **Reliable Transportation.** You need to plan for reliable transportation. It's not your employer's fault if your car won't start. You are still responsible for getting to work. Transportation problems can occur even if you own a new car. Here are a number of plans that you can make to ensure that you have reliable transportation.

- **Regular Car Maintenance.** Keep your car in good operating condition. Maintain it regularly. If you suspect you might have car trouble, try starting it a couple of hours before work. This will give you time to use another method of transportation if you need to.

- **Know Your Public Transportation System.** Keep a schedule of the public transportation available to you. Highlight the times that you would need to use the bus, train, or subway to get to work.

- **Call a Co-worker for a Ride.** Make friends with others at work. Find someone who lives near you and has a reliable car. Make an agreement with them to share a ride if either of you has car trouble. You may want to carpool with other co-workers.

- **Ride Sharing.** Check with friends or advertise in the classifieds for someone who can share a ride to work with you. This arrangement will work even when you don't work together. You just need to work in the same general area.

- **Walk or Bicycle.** Find housing near your place of employment. Even if you live two to four miles from your job, you can still walk or ride a bike in good weather. If you don't want to move, find a job near your home.

- **Taxis.** A taxi is costly, but it usually won't cost as much as losing a day's pay. It is even less costly than losing your job. You don't want to take a taxi to work every day, but you shouldn't hesitate to do so in an emergency.

2. **Reliable Child Care.** If you are responsible for children, you need reliable child care. What happens if a baby-sitter lets you down? What if bad weather closes a day-care center? What if your child is ill? What if children can't get to school on the normal schedule? You can make successful plans for child care that can help you avoid missing work by doing some detective work first.

   - **Hire Good Baby-Sitters.** Select a reliable baby-sitter. You can check reliability by asking for the baby-sitter's references. These should be people who have employed the person as a baby-sitter for their children.

   - **Select Good Child Care Centers.** Check on the child care center. Ask for references. Learn about their policy for closing. What is their policy if your child is ill? There are now more centers who will care for children when they are ill.

   - **Investigate Health Care Programs.** In some cases, hospitals and specialized child care centers will take care of your children when they are ill. Many of these programs only need to be used when your child is sick. They cost more than normal child care. However, they are less costly than an unpaid day off work or losing your job.

   - **Have an Emergency Plan.** Find a friend or relative who is willing to take care of your child for one day in case of emergency. The best plan is to have at least two people who are willing to do this.

3. **Use a Calendar.** Have a calendar and use it to keep track of your work schedule. Record all assigned work days and any personal appointments that may conflict with work. Doctor and dental appointments can be noted in time to make arrangements with your employer. Whenever possible, schedule personal appointments outside regular work hours.

- You may also want to note other personal business on your calendar. A calendar is one of the best tools to help you plan your work day. Use the forms that follow to plan your weekly and monthly schedule.

Weekly Planner

MONDAY   Date: _____

  Time   Appointment/Notes

_____ _____
_____ _____
_____ _____
_____ _____
_____ _____
_____ _____

TUESDAY   Date: _____

  Time   Appointment/Notes

_____ _____
_____ _____
_____ _____
_____ _____
_____ _____
_____ _____

WEDNESDAY Date: _____

  Time   Appointment/Notes

_____ _____
_____ _____
_____ _____
_____ _____
_____ _____
_____ _____

Weekly Planner

THURSDAY   Date: _____

  Time   Appointment/Notes

_____   _____
_____   _____
_____   _____
_____   _____
_____   _____
_____   _____

FRIDAY   Date: _____

  Time   Appointment/Notes

_____   _____
_____   _____
_____   _____
_____   _____
_____   _____
_____   _____

SATURDAY   Date: _____

  Time   Appointment/Notes

_____   _____
_____   _____
_____   _____
_____   _____
_____   _____
_____   _____

SUNDAY   Date: _____

  Time   Appointment/Notes

_____   _____
_____   _____
_____   _____
_____   _____
_____   _____
_____   _____

Monthly Calendar						
Month:						
Mon	**Tues**	**Wed**	**Thurs**	**Fri**	**Sat**	**Sun**

4. **Plan a Schedule with Your Supervisor.** You can plan for many events in your life — vacations, car maintenance, dental, doctor and lawyer appointments, to name a few. A supervisor can usually schedule a one-day absence with just a few weeks notice. A vacation may require several months notice. Ask your supervisor how much notice is needed to schedule days off.

5. **Call the Employer.** Even the best planning can't cover all possible problems that could keep you from getting to work. Your employer will usually understand if you only miss work once in a while. Ask your supervisor how many days is considered reasonable to be absent from work each year. Most organizations will take disciplinary action for excessive or unexcused absences. Disciplinary action may be taken for weekly absences, one absence every two weeks or on a day before or after a holiday, and for not calling in or taking off to do personal business. The discipline may range from a verbal warning for the first offense to immediate discharge.[5] Call your supervisor as soon as you know it will not be possible to get to work. Use a pay phone or a neighbor's phone if you don't have your own phone. Be honest and plan what you will say.

1. What will you tell your supervisor when you call?

   _____

   _____

   _____

Notifying Your Supervisor

When you notify your supervisor that you can't be at work, follow these steps:

- Identify yourself and state that you can't come to work.
- Explain the reason you can't be at work. Don't lie.
- If you expect to be gone for more than one day, tell the supervisor how long you expect to be away from the job.
- Express your willingness to make up for the absence when you return by making up the hours you missed.

Applying What You've Learned

There are good and bad reasons for being absent from work. Review the following list. Check those reasons you think justify calling your supervisor to say you can't come to work.

___ I have a headache and don't feel like coming to work.

___ My child is ill and I have to stay home.

___ My car isn't working and I don't have a ride to work.

___ I have the flu.

___ I have an appointment with my attorney.

___ There's been a death in my family.

___ My brother asked me to baby-sit his children.

___ I had a fight with my spouse and I am too upset to work.

___ I sprained my ankle and need to keep it elevated.

___ I need to visit a sick friend in the hospital.

___ Our house was broken into last night.

___ I need to get a new pair of glasses today.

___ I had a car accident on the way to work.

___ It was a long weekend and I have a hangover.

___ This is a religious holiday for me.

You should always tell the truth when you report to your supervisor. It is the right thing to do. A lie may be discovered and cause you embarrassment. It will take a long time to regain your supervisor's trust if you are discovered in a lie concerning your absence.

The Friday/Monday Syndrome

Supervisors recognize a pattern that develops among some employees. It frequently appears in younger workers. The syndrome becomes apparent when people call with an excuse not to come to work on a Friday or Monday. This problem worker is eager to start the weekend and when Monday rolls around is either too tired or needs time off to do personal business because they partied all weekend. Even when you have a legitimate excuse, supervisors will become irritated when most of your absences occur on Fridays and Mondays.

Getting to Work on Time

The same problems caused for an employer by absenteeism are caused by tardiness. There are reasonable causes for being late; however, more than once a month or four or five times a year is considered excessive by some employers. You need to plan ahead to be on time. Here are some suggestions to help you accomplish this.

- **A Reliable Alarm Clock.** You must have a reliable alarm clock. If you have an electric clock, make sure it has a back-up power source or use a wind-up clock as well in case the electricity shuts off. If you can't afford to buy one, borrow the money. You can't afford to lose a job because you don't get to work on time. Don't rely on someone else to get you up in time to get to work.

- **Get Up Early.** Allow yourself enough time to get ready and get to work. Plan enough time to eat breakfast and for transportation delays. You should also plan to arrive at work 8 to 10 minutes early. This cushion will help you mentally prepare for work and reduce stress. It also shows your supervisor you are eager to work.

- **Plan for Special Conditions.** There will be times when you can anticipate special conditions in which you'll need more time to get to work. For example, poor weather conditions means traffic will be slower. Get up earlier so you will still arrive on time.

- **Notify Your Supervisor if You Are Delayed.** Unless you will be less than 15 minutes late, notify your supervisor. You should give the following information:

  —Tell why you are going to be late.

  —Explain what you are doing to get to work as soon as possible.

  —Estimate when you will arrive.

  —Assure your supervisor you will make up the time.

Applying What You've Learned

Read the two situations described below. Explain how you would improve each situation.

Case Study 1

Buster was absent for two days from his job as a production worker at a shoe factory. When he returned, his supervisor, Mr. Brown, was angry. "Why didn't you call to let me know you weren't coming in to work?" Buster was surprised and answered, "My father-in-law died and we had to attend the funeral." Mr. Brown replied, "I'm sorry about your father-in-law, but I'm going to issue you a written warning. If this ever happens again you'll be fired."

1. Why do you think Mr. Brown reacted this way?

   _____

   _____

2. How could Buster have avoided this problem?

_____

_____

Case Study 2

Vanessa went to a party on Thursday night even though she had to go to work at 7:30 a.m. the following morning. She overslept on Friday morning and got to work 45 minutes late. Two weeks earlier she had gone to a party on Sunday and gotten drunk. She skipped work the next day. One week ago she was 20 minutes late because she had to pick up a friend and take her to work. Her supervisor warned her then not to be late for work. When Vanessa got to the office on Friday, the receptionist told her that her supervisor wanted to see her immediately.

1. What do you think her supervisor will say?

_____

_____

2. What should Vanessa do to keep her job and avoid this situation in the future?

_____

_____

Summary

In this chapter you've learned why employers need dependable workers. Good workers are important to an effective operation. That is why good attendance and punctuality are important to your employer. You'll find that a little planning and self-discipline will make it possible for you to be a dependable worker. Your supervisor will appreciate dependability. Many organizations encourage good attendance and punctuality through raises, bonuses, and promotions. It is to your benefit to be a dependable employee.

Chapter Four Endnotes

1. "Qualities Employers Like and Dislike in Job Applicants," *The Advisory Council for Technical-Vocational Education in Texas*, (Austin, Texas, 1975).

2. Tom Peters and Robert Waterman, *In Search of Excellence: Lessons from America's Best Run Companies*, (Warner Books, New York, 1982).

3. Peter G. Hanson, M.D., *Stress for Success: How to Make Stress on the Job Work for You*, (Doubleday, New York, 1989).

4. "On the Money," *Reader's Digest*, March 1990, 17.

5. Randall Schuler and Vandra Huber, *Personnel and Human Resource Management*, (West Publishing Company, St. Paul, Minn., 1990), 345-346.

Chapter Five
Learning to Do Your Job

WHAT'S IT ALL ABOUT?

A basic skill to acquiring all other skills is knowing how to learn. You spend the early years of your life learning in school. School provides a very structured approach to learning. Sometimes people think they only learn when they go to school, but we learn in a variety of ways. We watch other people doing something and do what they do. For example, you probably learned how to add gas and oil to a car by watching someone else do it. We ask other people how to do something like get a concert ticket. We also learn by reading books and magazines. If you want to wear the latest styles, you might buy a magazine that shows you what the current fashions are. By now you get the idea. There are a number of ways we can learn besides formal schooling.

Thinking About Learning

You will be required to learn many things at your new job. In this chapter you will explore ways to improve your learning skills while you do your new job. But don't think learning ends when you've mastered the new job. In time, your job will require new abilities, or you may want a promotion that requires additional skills. This chapter will help you understand how you can continue to learn new skills throughout your lifetime.

School is only one way we learn about things. The following exercise is designed to help you think about and understand the many other ways that you can learn. As you are doing this exercise, consider how the same steps you took in your learning project could help you learn new skills at work.

1. Write down something you learned outside of school within the last three months. (We'll refer to this as a learning project.)

   _____

   _____

   _____

   _____

2. List the steps that you went through during your learning project.

   _____

   _____

   _____

   _____

3. Was your learning project successful? Why or why not?

   _____

   _____

   _____

4. Are there other ways you could have learned the same thing? Explain how this could have been done.

   _____

   _____

   _____

   _____

Learning How to Do Your Job

To be successful in a job you must do it correctly. This statement seems obvious but it is not always easy to follow. It is essential that you know what the job tasks are and how to perform them, as well as how your work will be evaluated. How do you get this information?

1. List some of the things you can do to find out how to perform your job effectively. The items on your list could include things you would expect your supervisor to tell you about your job.

_____

_____

_____

_____

Where to Find Information About Your Job

There are many ways to find out how to do your job. Several proven methods are discussed below. Read and compare this material to your list above.

- **Job Descriptions.** Many employers will give you a job description. A job description is basically a written profile of the job. It should include all tasks and responsibilities for your job, but you will still need additional information to do your job well. Ask your supervisor to explain the job description to you. Make sure you really understand your responsibilities.

- **Training.** Businesses spend almost as much money each year to train employees as elementary and high schools and colleges spend to educate students.[1] You can expect to receive some sort of training when you begin a job. There are two basic types of training employers use:

  1. **On-the-job training.** This is usually one-on-one instruction that takes place as you do the job. Typically your supervisor will explain what to do, show you how to do it, watch while you practice, and then tell you how well you did in practice.

  2. **Classroom instruction.** Classroom instruction involves training several employees at the same time. There are many methods used in classroom instruction such as lecture, videos, discussion, role play, case studies, games, and learning exercises. It is important during any type of training to listen carefully and ask questions when you don't understand something.

- **Supervisors.** Supervisors should explain what they expect, but they may forget to tell you something. That is why it is important for you to ask for an explanation of your job if one is not given. While the job description explains the tasks you are to do, it doesn't give you all the details. Supervisors will help you understand exactly how the task should be done and more importantly, how they will evaluate your performance.

- **Co-workers.** Watch other workers who do the same job and note how they complete their tasks. They may have insight into how to do the job easier and how the supervisor expects the job to be done. Maybe someone was promoted from the job you now have. Talk with that person. Find out how they did the job. Their promotion probably means they did the job well. Listen carefully to what they say.

- **Friends.** Talk with friends and acquaintances who work at jobs similar to yours. Ask them how they do their jobs. You might get some good ideas to apply to your job. However, it is very important that you talk with your supervisor before trying out any of their suggestions.

- **Schools.** There are often classes you can take to learn more about your job. These classes are usually offered through adult education or continuing education programs at high schools or colleges. Some employers will help pay the cost because they know they will benefit from your skills. If, for example, you work with personal computers, you can probably enroll in a local computer class.

- **Reading.** Read about your job. There are general publications like the *Dictionary of Occupational Titles, Exploring Careers,* and *Occupational Outlook Handbook* that provide general occupational descriptions. These resources are good for workers just starting in a new occupation. You should be able to find these and other occupational books and magazines in your local library.

You want to be the best worker possible, so use all the sources listed above as well as any other ideas you have. Compare the resources discussed here with the list of steps you took on page 68 to learn something new.

1. List the recources you used from above.

   _____   _____

   _____   _____

   _____   _____

   _____   _____

2. What resources did you use that aren't listed above?

   _____   _____

   _____   _____

   _____   _____

   _____   _____

Applying What You've Learned

Knowing how to do your job right is essential to your job success. Below are two cases that describe the experience of workers in their new jobs. Read the cases and answer the questions that follow.

Case Study 1

Marc just began working as a computer operator at a large accounting firm. He has a computer technology diploma from a technical school. This is his first job. He has never worked with the IBM AS-400 computer that the company uses. His supervisor told him that they will provide on-the-job training. On his first day at work, Marc's supervisor said he was busy and showed Marc how to back up disk drives with the high speed tape drive. He then told Marc to spend the rest of the day doing backups.

1. If you were Marc, what would you do to find out more about the job you were hired to do?

   _____

   _____

   _____

   _____

Case Study 2

Paula has been on her new job as a receptionist for a week. Her supervisor told her that she is to provide clerical support for several staff members in the real estate office. This morning Susan asked her to file some house listings. While Paula was doing that, Karin asked her to type a letter. She had just started typing the letter when John told her to stop typing the letter and immediately prepare a contract. As Paula was preparing the contract she was interrupted by several phone calls. Karin came to get the letter and was upset because it wasn't finished. Just then John came out of his office and began to argue with Karin, telling her to let Paula finish the contract.

1. If you were Paula, how would you feel?

   _____

   _____

   _____

2. What information does Paula need to help her in this type of situation? How would she get the information she needs?

   _____

   _____

   _____

Continuing the Learning Process

You will always learn new things about your job. New machines may be installed. Policies and procedures may change. A new product may be manufactured and sold. The point is that all businesses are subject to change. As the business changes, so will your job. It is necessary for you to understand how you learn and to practice those techniques.

Education for Life

You may think your education is complete when you finish school. That assumption is far from true. You will need to continue to learn throughout your life. Futurist John Naisbitt wrote, "There is no one education, no one skill, that lasts a lifetime now."[2] When you start a new job you start learning all over again. You must learn how the organization operates and how to perform your job. Many organizations provide ongoing training. If your employer does not provide training to keep your skills current, consider getting trained on your own. It will help you stay competitive in today's job market. You are responsible for your lifelong education. You can participate in company training, continuing education classes, college classes, seminars and conferences to improve your job skills.

You will learn more when you understand your preferred method of learning. Everyone has a learning style.[3] Your style is determined by the ways you prefer to learn something new.

In the checklist below, rank from 1 (most preferred) to 7 (least preferred), the ways you prefer to learn.

_____**Reading.** Learn by reading and writing.

_____**Listening.** Learn by listening to lectures, tapes, or records.

_____**Observing.** Learn by looking at demonstrations, videos, films, slides, etc.

_____**Talking.** Learn by talking with other people, such as discussions or question and answer sessions.

_____**Doing.** Learn by actually doing what you are trying to learn, like building models or sketching.

_____**Participating.** Learn by participating in games, role plays, and other activities.

_____**Smelling/Tasting.** Learn by associating what you are learning with a smell or taste.

1. Look at how you ranked the methods. Now list the three learning methods you like best and use most frequently.

   1. _____

   2. _____

   3. _____

These three methods show your learning style. You may like reading and observing, or prefer listening and talking. You may learn by doing, participating, and smelling or tasting. Or you may use all of these senses. There are other ways to determine how you learn. Tests such as the Myers-Briggs Type Indicator can help you determine more about your learning style.[4]

It is important that you understand the ways you learn best. This can help you become a better learner. When you are faced with learning a new task, try to use your preferred learning methods. If you like "doing" then you will not learn as well if you try to learn by "reading." However, there are times when we must use a method not of our choosing. When this happens, do your best to use the required method and try to use your preferred style to review what you have learned.

Steps to Learning

Although everyone has their own learning style, there are some specific steps you can take to improve the way you learn. At the beginning of this chapter, you completed an exercise about something that you recently learned outside of school. This was called your learning project. The term "learning project" simply means the process of learning something new. The steps to complete a learning project are explained below. You probably listed some of these steps earlier.

Step 1. Motivate Yourself. You must find something exciting and interesting about your learning project. If you aren't interested in the subject itself, you might be more interested in something that could result from what you learn. For example, learning to fill out a new form required for your job may not excite you, but you might get excited about getting a raise because you do such a good job of completing the form. Write down your reasons for wanting to complete a learning project before you start the process.

Step 2. Set Objectives. The final outcomes of learning are called objectives. You need to know your learning objectives. Ask yourself the following question to identify your objectives. "When I am done with a learning project what must I be able to do?" Write down these objectives. Remember to be specific and state what you want to be able to do when the learning project is completed.

Step 3. Identify Resources. Find out what resources are available to help you reach your learning objectives. These resources may come from several areas.

- **In-house Learning Opportunities.** Ask your supervisor if your employer offers any courses that may help you meet your learning objectives. Perhaps there is another worker who can teach you what you want to learn.

- **Outside Education.** Ask someone in your organization (training manager, human resources manager, personnel director, or supervisor) to help you find out what courses are offered in vocational schools, community colleges, universities, and specialized training firms in your community.

- **Additional Methods.** Discuss your learning needs with friends and co-workers. Find out what methods they have used to learn something similar. Find out what kinds of books, educational videotapes or audio tapes are available at your library.

Step 4. Choose the Best Resources. You need to decide which of the resources you identify will help you the most in completing your learning project. You may decide to use more than one resource. Another factor to consider is cost. Find out if your employer will pay for the cost of any of these resources and if you will be allowed to take time from work if necessary. Also keep in mind that other people are an important resource for any learning project.[5]

Step 5. Schedule the Project. Once you select the resource(s) that you will use, schedule your project. Plan the time needed for your project and decide when you want to complete it. If you need to take time from work for this project, discuss the matter with your supervisor.

Step 6. Write Down Questions. Decide what questions you need to answer to learn the task. Write the questions down on a piece of paper. Check the questions off as you find the answer to them. Questions should ask who, what, where, when, why and how. These are the classic questions used by journalists to find answers.

Step 7. Complete the Project. Completing any learning project requires self-discipline. You must follow through with the plan that you created. It may be helpful to find someone who will keep you on track by checking your progress.

Step 8. Evaluate Progress. As you complete the learning project, evaluate your progress. Is the resource(s) you decided to use providing you with the knowledge and skills you need? Are you following the schedule you set? Are you getting the skills and knowledge that you set as your objective? Have an experienced person test your new skills and knowledge. Remember, the most important step to successful learning is completing the objective.

Step 9. Practice. The most effective way to become more skilled is to practice what you've learned even after the learning project is complete. Constantly check yourself on how well you can apply your new knowledge.

Personal Learning Project

This exercise is designed to help you put into practice the steps needed to complete a learning project.

1. Select a skill you want to learn and write it below.

   _____

2. What is your motivation? Why do you want to learn this skill? How do you think you will feel after learning it?

   _____

   _____

   _____

   _____

   _____

©1992, JIST Works, Inc. • Indianapolis, Indiana

3. Decide on a learning objective. What are your expected outcomes?

_____

_____

_____

_____

_____

4. Who could help you plan your learning project?

_____

_____

_____

5. What resources could you use to complete your learning project?

_____

_____

_____

_____

_____

6. What do you think would be your best resource? Keep in mind learning style, cost, availability, etc.

_____

_____

_____

_____

_____

7. When would you like to complete the learning project?

_____

8. How much time will you spend daily or weekly on the project?

_____

9. How will you evaluate your progress?

_____

_____

_____

_____

_____

10. How will you practice what you learn?

_____

_____

_____

_____

_____

Applying What You've Learned

The ability to learn is the most important skill that you can possess. Once you have mastered this skill, it is possible to develop other skills you need. Successful people know how to learn new things. Read the following case studies and develop a plan for each person to learn a new skill. Be specific about the steps for each learning project. Use more paper if necessary.

Case Study 1

Donna has spent the last four months working at Quick Print Shop. She runs a copy machine for orders of 500 copies or less. Donna has decided that she would like to learn more about graphic arts. She'd like to be able to run an offset press that is used for larger orders and those that require more complex printing techniques.

1. What do you think Donna should do to learn this new skill?

_____

_____

_____

_____

_____

Case Study 2

Juan works as a bank teller. He would like to work in the accounting department which would mean a higher salary. He knows that if he knew more about accounting he would have a better chance at a promotion to that area.

1. What should Juan do to learn more about accounting?

_____

_____

_____

_____

_____

Summary

On-the-job learning is an important skill to master. Training you receive on the job accounts for 85 percent of the income that you will earn in your lifetime.[6] You need to know how to take advantage of such training so you can learn new skills. Keep in mind that there will be many times you must learn on your own. Several ways to learn on your own have been presented in this chapter. The more you practice learning, the better your learning skills will be.

Chapter Five Endnotes

1. Anthony Carnevale, Leila Gainer and Janice Villet, *Training In America*, (Jossey-Bass, San Francisco, 1990).

2. John Naisbitt, and Patricia Aburdene, *Re-inventing The Corporation*, (Warner Books, Inc., New York, 1985).

3. Robert Smith, *Learning How To Learn*, (Follet Publishing Company, Chicago, 1983).

4. Katherine Briggs, and Isabel Briggs-Myers, Myers Briggs Type Indicator, (Consulting Psychologists Press, Palo Alto, Calif., 1987).

5. Stephen Brookfield, (Ed.), *Self-Directed Learning: From Theory to Practice*, (Jossey-Bass, San Francisco, 1985).

6. "Serving The New Corporation", *American Society for Training and Development*, (Alexandria, Va., 1986).

Chapter Six
Knowing Yourself

Your Self-Concept

According to research, employers want employees with positive self-concepts[1] Higher morale, more motivation and greater productivity are indications of a positive self-concept.[2] Because productivity, work quality, creativity and flexibility are based on self-concepts, a positive self-concept affects your job success.

To be a good employee, you must believe you are a good employee. In other words, you must have confidence in yourself. Your confidence comes from your self-concept , which is a mixture of your self-image (how you see yourself) and self-esteem (how you feel about your self-image). Let's look at how each of these affect the way you approach a job.

How Your Self-Image Affects Your Work Relationships

Perhaps you know someone who isn't all that great looking, but because they think they are or act like they are, they really are great looking. Other people really can see their beauty. A positive self- image can turn an "ugly duckling into a beautiful swan." On the other hand, a beautiful swan with a poor self-image could just as easily go unnoticed and unappreciated their entire life.

Your self-image is influenced by many people.[3] Parents influence how you view yourself. Many adults admit they still feel an urge to "please Mom and Dad." Your brothers and sisters are often your most willing critics. Teachers and supervisors evaluate you. You may feel a certain grade is a statement of your personal worth. Peers influence how you act, what you wear and even where you go. A legitimate fear is that if you don't meet your friends' standards you will be the next recipient of "The Nerd of the Year Award."

The good news is that the single, most important influence of your self-image is YOU. How you feel about any facet of yourself makes up your self-esteem. You can't be negative unless you choose to be negative. By learning to know and value yourself, you can choose to have a positive self-image.

Other Influences on Your Self-Concept

Another factor of your self-concept is self-awareness. (Self-image and self-esteem alone are not totally descriptive of self-concept.) As in the earlier example, you may be a physically beautiful person whose self-esteem has suffered because you are unaware of your beauty.

A positive self-concept is reflected in work relationships. The ability to communicate with your supervisor, co-workers and customers is extremely important. If you do not view yourself in a positive way, these relationships may be hindered. In this chapter we'll explore ways you can improve your self-awareness and create a positive self-concept.

Applying What You've Learned

Case Study 1

Corey works at the Speedi-In Deli. He began working after school hours one year ago. His job involves stocking shelves, keeping the pop machines filled and general clean-up chores. Corey works fairly independently. He enjoys his job, but feels he would like to advance to a behind-the-counter job. Although Corey doesn't have a positive self-image, he believes he could do this job.

The deli manager is extremely pleased with Corey's work. On Friday, he put this note in Corey's pay envelope, "Great job! Looking forward to advancing you."

On Monday, Corey and the manager are the only people working in the stockroom. The manager doesn't say anything about the note, but seems to be expecting a response from Corey. Because Corey doesn't feel good about himself, he feels uncomfortable accepting the manager's praise. He doesn't know what to say.

1. How do you think Corey's manager will react if Corey doesn't say anything?

    _____

    _____

    _____

2. Do you think this will affect Corey's opportunity to be promoted to the counter job? Explain?

    _____

    _____

    _____

3. How will your answer to question 2 affect Corey's self-concept?

    _____

    _____

    _____

Case Study 2

Dani had a speech problem as a young child. She was often teased because of it. Speech therapy in elementary school helped Dani overcome her handicap. Although she no longer has the speech problem, Dani is not confident in social conversations. She doesn't look at the person she is speaking to and sometimes mumbles.

Dani works at the Burger Bash. She spends her entire shift in the kitchen as fry cook and would like another job at the restaurant. Dani knows that one of the cashiers is quitting at the end of the school year to attend college. She really wants the cashier's job, but is afraid her poor communication skills will hinder her chance of promotion.

Dani decides to overcome this obstacle. At first, she practices simple conversations with friends and co-workers. She even makes a special effort to talk to some of her teachers and an elderly neighbor. She also takes a public speaking course at school. When her Burger Bash supervisor has team meetings, Dani answers questions and even jokes with the group. Gradually, she feels better about talking in social situations.

1. How do you think Dani's actions will affect her chances of becoming a cashier?

    _____

    _____

    _____

2. How do you think Dani's self-concept was affected by her actions? Explain the reason for your answer.

_____

_____

_____

Difficulties in the work place like Corey and Dani experienced create job stress. Not only will your job be more enjoyable if you approach it in a positive way, you reduce your job stress. This positive approach begins with a positive self-image, which enhances your confidence to do the job. After all, your employer hired you because he believes you are qualified to do the work. Your employer believes in you.

Learn to Believe in Yourself

Sometimes it may seem like everyone else at work but you knows what they are doing. That's not true. No one always feels confident. Anyone can experience a poor self-image, especially when circumstances change abruptly. For example:

- A teacher loses her job because there is no money to fund the gifted program for the coming year. She questions her ability to find a new teachning position. She wants to try a new area of work, but wonders if she is really qualified to enter a new field. Her indecision is caused by a sudden lack of confidence.

- A man is laid off after working 23 years in the same manufacturing plant. Rumors are the plant will soon close and move to a new location. Questions run through his mind, "Should I move my family to the new plant location? Should I start that auto repair shop I've always dreamed about? What if I can't pay all the bills?" He has trouble deciding what to do.

- Your supervisor is asked to move up in the company. She currently has 10 employees reporting to her. She would be responsible for 25 workers if she accepts the new position. The hours are the same and the pay is better. But, she needs to take a computer course at the local university to work in the new area. She begins to question her abilities. "Can I handle a college course? I haven't attended a university class in 10 years. What if I can't pass the course? What if I can't operate the computer? Can I really supervise 25 people? Maybe I'm not ready for a promotion just yet."

Having a positive self-concept doesn't mean you won't ever question yourself. In fact, the questions these people asked are healthy questions. Questioning allows you to compare your self-image with the world around you. You don't want to put yourself in a position where you can't perform well because you inaccurately evaluated your skills and abilities. This is why self-awareness is so important. It allows you to make better decisions about your career and how to perform on a job.

How You Look at Life

According to scientists who study personalities, people approach life in one of two ways. They either feel they control their lives or else other people and things control them.[4] The way you look at life greatly affects your self-concept. The following quiz will help you understand how you view your control over your life.

Answer the following questions. In the "Answer" column, put a "T" beside the statements you think are true and an "F" beside those you think are false.

Your Approach To Life Quiz		
VIEWS OF LIFE	**ANSWER**	**SCORE**
1. Other people control my life.		
2. I am responsible for the success in my life.		
3. Success in life is a matter of luck.		
4. When things go wrong it's usually because of things I couldn't control.		
5. The last time I did something successful I knew it was successful because of my own efforts.		
6. The last time I failed at something I knew it was because I just wasn't good enough to get the job done.		
7. Most successful people are born successful.		
8. It seems that most things are beyond my control.		
9. When I fail, it is usually someone else's fault.		
10. When I succeed, it is usually because of someone else's efforts.		
SCORE		
TOTAL SCORE		

Scoring:

Statement 1, True = 0, False = 1
Statement 2, True = 1, False = 0
Statement 3, True = 0, False = 1
Statement 4, True = 0, False = 1
Statement 5, True = 1, False = 0

Statement 6, True = 0, False = 1
Statement 7, True = 0, False = 1
Statement 8, True = 0, False = 1
Statement 9, True = 0, False = 1
Statement 10, True = 0, False = 1

Interpretation: Score and View of Life

0 - 3, Outside My Control — I'm not responsible for my successes or my failures. I need to work on my self-concept.

4 - 6, Sometimes in Control — I'm sometimes responsible for my successes and failures. My self-concept could be improved.

7 - 10, In Control — I'm responsible for my successes. I have confidence in myself and have a good self-concept.

You Can Teach Yourself to View Life Positively

People with positive self-concepts look at their successes and believe they are responsible for them. These people also believe that while they are responsible for their failures, events, things and people outside their control also affected the outcome. People with negative self-concepts view the world exactly opposite. They credit their successes to luck and never accept the blame for their failures. Thus, they fail to accept responsibility for their own actions. Those in the "Outside My Control" category in the previous quiz need to work harder to develop a positive self-concept while those in the "In Control" category find it easier to develop a positive self-concept.

Like anything else, this approach to life can be taken to extremes. There are times when your success is due to luck and failure is solely your own fault. But by being realistic about your personal contributions to success and failure, you'll know how to improve yourself. Most importantly, you need to believe that you can improve. In fact, you can overcome any problem or difficulty given enough time, effort, and when needed, help from other people. The important thing is to have faith in yourself.

You can teach yourself how to view life more positively and be "in control" of your own life.[5] Look at the circumstances every time you succeed. Give yourself credit for success. Remember to look at the small successes that occur everyday of your life. Similarly, when you experience failure, examine the reason for the failure. Look for those outside factors that contributed to the failure and realize how they affected the outcome. In the next exercise you will look at the successes and failures in your life and see how you personally contribute to your successes.

Selling Yourself on You

Joe Girard was the best car salesman in the world for eight years in a row, selling more than 11,200 cars. He was successful because he believed in himself. He gives these tips for improving self-image.[6]

- Tell yourself you are number one every morning.
- Write "I believe in myself" on cards and place them where you'll see them frequently throughout the day.
- Associate with other winners and avoid losers.
- Put negative thoughts like envy, jealousy, greed and hate out of your life.
- Pat yourself on the back at least once a day.
- Repeat "I will" at least 10 times each day.
- Do the things you fear most to prove you can successfully accomplish them.

Personal Evaluation Exercise

1. List three successes you had during the past week.

   _____

   _____

   _____

2. How were you responsible for making each success happen?

   _____

   _____

   _____

   _____

   _____

   _____

3. List three failures you had during the past week.

   _____

   _____

   _____

4. Explain what outside factors contributed to each failure.

   _____

   _____

   _____

   _____

   _____

There are some important things to learn from this exercise. First, we all have successes in our lives. You should take the credit and reward yourself for them. Second, we all have failures in our lives, but every failure can be overcome. Analyze the reason for the failure. Was it really your fault or the result of something you couldn't anticipate? Look at failure as an opportunity to learn from mistakes and avoid repeating them in the future. As you apply these principles in your life you can learn to take control and develop a more positive self-concept.

Your Job and Your Self-Concept

When life experiences make you doubt yourself, a positive self-image can help you continue to believe in your abilities. You face unique challenges in the work world. Many job-related situations are totally new to you. For instance, perhaps you're starting a new job. You may question your ability to complete your assigned tasks. But it is important to remember that as you gain experience you will develop more confidence. To protect your positive self-image as you begin your new job, try to remember these two simple facts.

FACT 1 — You will make mistakes. When you make mistakes, acknowledge them. Accept any criticism or advice from your supervisor and correct the mistake. For each mistake, examine the situation and note the contributing factors. Decide how you can avoid the same mistake in the future. This way you learn from your mistakes. You will know you're capable of improving and your self-image is positively reinforced.

FACT 2 — Your employer wants you to succeed. Employers do not hire people in order to fire them. Your employer evaluated your skills and chose you for the job because he believes you have the ability to do the job successfully. Your employer has confidence in you. Give yourself credit for your accomplishments. Learn to accept compliments gracefully. When you are complimented on your work, simply say "thank you." If your supervisor or co-workers neglect to compliment you, compliment yourself!

Identifying Your Skills

Take an honest look at yourself. You may be surprised at the variety of skills you can offer an employer. You develop skills from all your life experiences. The exercises in this section are adapted from *A Young Person's Guide to Getting and Keeping a Good Job* by Mike Farr and Marie Pavlicko.[7] They are designed to help you become more aware of your job-related skills which are divided into three categories:

- Self-Management skills
- Transferable skills
- Job-Related skills

Self-Management Skills

Self-management skills are related to the control you have over your life — how you plan, implement, change, and evelute the activities in your life. Some self-management skills are necessary to please your employer. You probably have some of these skills already. Your employer expects you to use these skills most of the time. While not all employers look for the same skills, the key self-management skills listed on the next page are highly valued by all employers.

Self-Management Skills Checklist

- Check all the following skills which apply to you.

Key Self-Management Skills

These are skills all employers value highly. They often won't hire a person who does not have or use most or all of these.

Employers Value People Who

Skill	Most Times	Some Times
get to work every day		
arrive on time		
get things done		
follow instructions from supervisor		

Skill	Most Times	Some Times
get along well with co-workers		
are honest		
work hard		

Other Self-Management Skills

Skill	Most Times	Some Times
ambition		
patience		
assertiveness		
learns quickly		
flexibility		
maturity		
dependability		
completes assignments		
sincerity		
solves problems		
friendliness		
a good sense of humor		
physical strength		

Skill	Most Times	Some Times
highly motivated		
intelligence		
creativity		
leadership		
enthusiasm		
persistence		
self-motivated		
results oriented		
pride in doing a good job		
willingness to learn new things		
takes responsibility		
asks questions		

Additional Self-Management Skills

- Add any self-management skills you have that are not on the list.

Skill	Most Times	Some Times

Skill	Most Times	Some Times

- Review the charts you just filled out.. Count the number of times you checked "Most Times" and "Some Times." Record the numbers below.

Self-Management Skills Record	
Most Times	
Some Times	
Total Skill Points	

Self-management skills help you change and succeed in unfamiliar situations. Some of these skills are a part of your personality. Others include your ability to get along with people and adapt to work situations.

Transferable Skills

Transferable skills are skills that can be used in many different jobs. A grocery store cashier needs to understand numbers, but so do bank tellers and accounting clerks. A nurse must have good people skills, as does a receptionist or a department store customer service representative. Employers value some transferable skills over others. The key transferable skills listed on the next page may help you get a higher paying job or a more responsible position, or both.

Transferable Skills Checklist

Key Transferable Skills

These skills tend to get you higher levels of responsibility and pay. They are worth emphasizing in an interview!

Skill	Most Times	Some Times
meet deadlines		
speak in public		
supervise others		
accept responsibility		

Skill	Most Times	Some Times
solve problems		
plan		
increase sales or efficiency		
instruct others		

Skill	Most Times	Some Times
manage money, budgets		
understand and control budgets		
manage people		

Skill	Most Times	Some Times
meet deadlines		
meet the public		
organize/manage projects		

Other Transferable Skills

Using My Hands/Dealing with Things

Skill	Most Times	Some Times
assemble		
build		
construct/repair buildings		
drive/operate vehicles		
good with hands		

Skill	Most Times	Some Times
observe/inspect		
operate tools, machines		
repair		
use complex equipment		
make things		

Dealing with Data

Skill	Most Times	Some Times
analyze data		
audit records		
budget		
calculate/compute		
check for accuracy		
classify data		
compare		
compile		
count		
detail-oriented		
evaluate		

Skill	Most Times	Some Times
investigate		
keep financial records		
locate answers, information		
manage money		
observe/inspect		
record facts		
negotiate		
research		
synthesize		
take inventory		

Working with People

Skill	Most Times	Some Times
administer		
care for		
confront others		
counsel people		
demonstrate		
diplomatic		
help others		
insight		
instruct		
interview people		
kind		
listen		
mentoring		

Skill	Most Times	Some Times
outgoing		
patient		
persuade		
pleasant		
sensitive		
sociable		
supervise		
tactful		
teach		
tolerant		
tough		
trust		
understand		

Using Words, Ideas

Skill	Most Times	Some Times
articulate		
communicate verbally		
correspond with others		
create new ideas		
design		
edit		

Skill	Most Times	Some Times
ingenious		
inventive		
library research		
logical		
public speaking		
remember information		
write clearly		

Leadership

Skill	Most Times	Some Times	Skill	Most Times	Some Times
arrange social functions			negotiate agreements		
competitive			plan		
decisive			results oriented		
delegate			risk taker		
direct others			run meetings		
explain things to others			self-confident		
mediate problems			self-motivated		
motivate people			solve problems		

Creative/Artistic

Skill	Most Times	Some Times	Skill	Most Times	Some Times
artistic			present artistic ideas		
drawing, art			dance, body movement		
expressive					
perform, act					

Other Transferable Skills

- Add any transferable skills you have that are not on the list.

Additional Transferable Skills

Skill	Most Times	Some Times	Skill	Most Times	Some Times

- Review the charts you filled out. Count the number of time you checked "Most Times" and "Some Times." Record the numbers on the following page.

Self-Management Skills Record	
Most Times	
Some Times	
Total Skill Points	

Job-Related Skills

You use job-related skills to do a particular job. For example, a truck driver must know how to drive a large truck and operate its gears. A paramedic must be able to take blood pressure and use a stethoscope. Some job-related skills are the result of years of training. Others may be learned in a short time.

If you have interest in a particular job, you probably have some skills necessary to do that job. These skills come from a variety of experiences including education, other jobs, volunteer work, hobbies, extracurricular activities and even family activities. Do the following exercise to see what skills you have that could be used in the job you want.

1. List the skills related to this job that you have gained from school courses or vocational training.

   _____   _____

   _____   _____

   _____   _____

2. List your skills related to this job that you gained from other jobs or volunteer work.

   _____   _____

   _____   _____

   _____   _____

3. List your skills related to this job that you gained from hobbies, family activities, extracurricular activities and other experiences outside of school or work.

   _____   _____

   _____   _____

   _____   _____

- Give yourself one point for each job-related skill you listed. Record that number in the box below.

TOTAL JOB-RELATED SKILLS	

A Review of Your Skills

- Add your total points for each skill area and write them in the appropriate spaces below. This shows you the variety of skills you have to offer an employer. You are a valuable member of your employer's team.

TOTAL Self-Management Skills	
TOTAL Transferable Skills	
TOTAL Job-Related Skills	

Identifying your skills will help you see your strongest points as an employee. Now that you know your skills, you can use them to improve your position in the work world. Is there a skill that you aren't using? Do you have a skill that is weak? How could you improve this skill?

1. Write a short statement explaining how you feel about yourself, now that you've identified your skills.

_____

_____

_____

_____

_____

Applying What You've Learned

Case Study 1

Darren works in a formal-wear store. Last week a wedding party of 10 came in to be measured for tuxedoes. Darren carefully measured each person and recorded the measurements on the proper form. When the groom became impatient with the long wait, Darren joked with him about the wedding. By the time the group left, the groom was smiling. Then Darren discovered that he had undercharged the group by $50.

1. What are Darren's stronger skills?

_____

_____

_____

2. What are Darren's weaker skills?

_____

_____

_____

3. How can Darren improve his weaker skills?

_____

_____

_____

Case Study 2

Sheila works in the university research library. A professor sent a list of research articles to be reserved for his classes. Sheila went through the stacks and pulled all but one of the requested articles. Although she was unable to find one article, she packaged the rest and sent them to the professor. Her supervisor did not okay the order. Later, the professor complained to Sheila's supervisor that his order was incomplete. The supervisor called Sheila into the office and explained the mistake. Sheila became very angry and left the office.

1. What are Sheila's stronger skills?

_____

_____

_____

2. What are Sheila's weaker skills?

_____

_____

_____

3. How can Sheila improve her weaker skills?

_____

_____

_____

Summary

Dieticians tell us "you are what you eat," to encourage us to develop healthy bodies through good nutrition. To develop a healthier self-image, an appropriate saying might be "you are what you think." In truth, if you believe you can do the job, you can do it. Here are some useful tips to help you believe in yourself.

- **Think positive.** Think success, not failure. Be your own cheerleader.

- **Accept compliments.** Learn to say a simple "thank you" when you are complimented.

- **Accept responsibility.** Learn to accept responsibility for your successes as well as your failures, but recognize how other factors contribute to failure. Be proud of your successes. Strive to improve your weaker skills and correct your mistakes.

- **Identify your skills.** Use your special abilities to help improve your skills and build up your positive self-concept.

- **Reward yourself.** Treat yourself for being successful. Buy something special to remember the occasion. Celebrate!

Chapter Six Endnotes

1. Anthony Carnevale, Leila Gainer, and Ann Meltzer, *Work Place Basics: The Essential Skills Employers Want*, (Jossey-Bass Publishers, San Francisco, 1990), 215-232.

2. Robert Baron, *Understanding Human Relations: A Practical Guide to People at Work*, (Allyn and Bacon, Inc., Boston, 1985), 165.

3. Jeffrey Turner and Donald Helms, *Life Span Development*, (W.B. Saunders Company, Philadelphia, 1979), 224-226.

4. Richard Daft and Richard Steers, *Organizations: A Micro/Macro Approach*, (Scott, Foresman and Co., Glenview, Ill., 1986), 72.

5. David Cherrington, Nyal McMullin and Betty McMullin, *Organizational Behavior*, (Allyn and Bacon, Boston, 1989), 106.

6. Joe Girard, *How to Sell Yourself*, (Warner Books, New York, 1979).

7. Michael Farr and Marie Pavlicko, *A Young Person's Guide to Getting and Keeping a Good Job*, (JIST Works, Inc., Indianapolis, 1990).

Chapter Seven

Getting Along with Your Supervisor

SUPERVISING IS A JOB

Your boss is your employer or supervisor. Thomas Von der Embse, described supervision, "In short, it is getting people to make what we have into what we want."[1] This means your supervisor not only wants, but needs your cooperation to get work done.

Your supervisor may or may not have hired you directly, but that person is the decision maker and that fact will affect your work experience. Supervisors frequently make recommendations about promotions, salary increases, and firing employees. It is important you get along with your supervisor. Cooperating will make your work experience more pleasant and help advance your career. It will also help you get a positive recommendation if you look for another job.

Your Supervisor Is the Team Leader in the Business World

In today's business world the supervisor plays a very important role. The supervisor is seen as a leader, coach, cheerleader, teacher, and counselor. That person plans, schedules, orders work materials, directs the activities of employees, checks the productivity and quality of work, and coordinates all work activities with other areas of the organization.

The supervisor is also responsible for leading work groups. Many organizations now refer to work groups as teams. You need to view yourself as a part of a team if you participate in a work group. Each worker must do their job correctly for the team to be successful. The supervisor delegates work to the members of your work group. Your supervisor depends on you to do your job and do it the right way.

Delegate

This term identifies the process where a supervisor assigns or distributes a task to an employee. It is necessary for a supervisor to delegate tasks to employees in order to get all the work done. When a task is delegated to you, be sure to follow instructions carefully. Periodically, report back to your supervisor to let them know how the job is progressing. Let your supervisor know when you are finished with an assigned task.

What Does a Supervisor Do?

Complete the following exercise to test your understanding of the responsibilities a supervisor might have. Place an A (Always) beside those tasks you think a supervisor would always do. Put S (Sometimes) beside those tasks that a supervisor would sometimes do and N (Never) beside those tasks you think a supervisor would never do.

- Matt is the owner-manager of a 24-hour self-service gas station.

    ____Order gasoline   ____ Train new employees

    ____Make out the payroll   ____ Arrange for police protection

    ____Schedule workers   ____ Pump gas

    ____Change oil   ____ Dismiss unacceptable employees

    1. Why did you rate these tasks the way you did?

    _____

    _____

    _____

- Krista is the supervisor of the make-up department in a local drug store.

  ___ Order make-up   ___ Balance the cash register

  ___ Handle customer complaints   ___ Evaluate employees

  ___ Stock the shelves   ___ Product demonstration

  ___ Distribute employee   ___ Return damaged products
       paychecks

  1. Why did you rate these tasks the way you did?

  _____

  _____

  _____

- Joel supervises a group of 15 telemarketing operators.

  ___ Settle employee   ___ Solve problems
       disagreements   ___ Make phone calls

  ___ Schedule vacations   ___ Repair electronic equipment

  ___ Listen to phone calls made by   ___ Answer customer questions
       employees

  ___ Track sales

  1. Why did you rate these tasks the way you did?

  _____

  _____

  _____

- Marta is a line supervisor of an electronic components assembly factory.

  ___ Check quality of finished   ___ Sign employees' paychecks
       items   ___ Evaluate workers' performances

  ___ Fill in for absent workers   ___ Inspect for safety violations

  ___ Set personnel policies   ___ Talk with union leaders

  ___ Keep a parts inventory

  1. Why did you rate these tasks the way you did?

  _____

  _____

  _____

- Jeff manages a frozen yogurt shop.

  ____Create new yogurt flavors   ____Conduct health department inspections

  ____Take customer orders

  ____Maintain equipment   ____Plan advertising

  ____Clean tables   ____Make bank deposits

  ____Bookkeeping

  1. Why did you rate these tasks the way you did?

  _____

  _____

  _____

It's Not as Easy as It Looks

An old folk tale tells the story of a husband and wife who traded jobs for a day. Each one thought they could do the other person's job quicker and better. Each planned an afternoon of leisure after a morning of efficient work.

The husband stayed home to do household chores, and his wife went off to the field. Neither did the other's job well. By the end of the day, the house was in total ruin, the dinner was burned, the cow was not milked nor was the field plowed. Totally exhausted after a frustrating day, they shared a cold dinner and agreed that neither job was easy. The next day they returned to their own work with much relief.

Some employees think supervising is easy. It is important that you realize supervisors have responsibilities that other employees don't have. Employees are often unaware of the stress this may cause supervisors. Your supervisor's outlook of the work day may be affected by this stress. Knowing this will help you respect your supervisor's job. The previous exercise was designed to help you understand how difficult a supervisor's job can be. Throughout this chapter you will learn how to get along with your supervisor and help your supervisor do an effective job.

Communicating with Your Supervisor

Communicating with your supervisor is important to both of you. There are five important aspects to remember when communicating with your supervisor:

1. You must be able to follow instructions.

2. You need to know how to ask questions.

3. You should report any problems and results of your work.

4. You need to accurately record and give messages to your supervisor.

5. You need to discuss your job performance.

Rely on Your Senses When Following Instructions

Following instructions is extremely important at all times, but especially during your training period. Your supervisor will be watching to see how well you do this. Use your senses to follow instructions correctly.

- **Concentrate.** Focus your attention on the supervisor. Don't be distracted by noise and movement.

- **Listen.** Pay attention to the words being spoken. If you hear unfamiliar words or terms, ask for clarification. Listening also means interpreting body language, voice inflections, and gestures. If this nonverbal communication is confusing, ask the supervisor to clarify what you don't understand.

- **Watch.** Sometimes a supervisor will demonstrate how a task is performed. If necessary, ask the supervisor to repeat the process until you understand it completely. Sometimes a task may be too complex or time-consuming to demonstrate. In such cases, you will probably receive general instructions. If there are details you don't understand, you need to ask for guidance to continue the task.

- **Question.** After you have listened and watched, ask questions. A good supervisor will encourage you to ask questions. It is better to ask a question than to make a mistake and use the excuse that you didn't understand.

- **Write.** Write down in a small notebook the important points to remember about the instructions you get. Don't write while your supervisor is talking or demonstrating something. Do it later.

- **Practice.** With your supervisor's permission, perform the task. Make sure you have fully completed the job. This may include putting tools away or cleaning up your work area. Don't leave your work only partially completed.

Jargon

Every organization develops its own words and terminology. This language is called "jargon." Jargon might be the most difficult thing for a new employee to learn. Jargon can be in the form of words or acronyms. For example, your supervisor may tell you that you will be "pulling" today. This could be an expression that means you'll be taking packages off a conveyor belt to be loaded into a truck. An acronym is an abbreviation of a phrase. If your supervisor says you can't get a computer until you submit an RFP, that may refer to "Request For Purchase." When you hear a term that is unclear, don't be afraid to ask for an explanation. Some organizations give new employees a booklet that defines terms unique to that business.

Understanding Instructions

This exercise is designed to help you understand how to follow instructions. Complete the following:

- Take a blank sheet of 8 1/2" x 11" paper.
- Fold the paper in half.
- Now fold the paper in half again.
- Fold the paper in half one more time.

There are two possibilities that can result from following these directions:

1. You could end up with a paper measuring 2-3/4" x 4-1/4" or

2. It could measure 2-1/4" x 5-1/2." The results differ because the instructions are not entirely clear, just as some instructions you receive from a supervisor may not be completely clear.

1. What questions could you have asked to better understand the instructions?

_____

_____

_____

2. How would you rewrite the instructions so there is only one possible outcome?

_____

_____

_____

Asking Questions

If you don't understand something, ask questions. Your supervisor can't read your mind. It's better to ask a question than to make a major mistake. Yet most people are reluctant to ask questions for fear of looking stupid. If this applies to you, you need to overcome your reluctance. Not asking questions could result in broken equipment, an angry customer or other mistakes that will negatively affect your performance rating. It may even cost you the job. Here are some simple guidelines for asking questions.

- **Ask Immediately.** You should ask the question as soon as it arises. The longer you wait the more irrelevant it will seem and you won't ask it at all.
- **Summarize the Response.** When your supervisor answers your question, repeat the answer in your own words. This helps you make sure that you clearly understand the answer.
- **Memorize the Answer.** It is irritating to answer the same question repeatedly. Your supervisor may grow impatient with you if this happens. Record answers in your notebook if you have trouble remembering them.

Reporting the Results

Your supervisor needs to be kept informed about your work. Sometimes the supervisor will be close enough to observe your work at all times, but this is not always the case. It would then be your responsibility to keep the supervisor informed about your work status. Advise your supervisor in the following situations.

- **When you complete a task.** The supervisor needs to know if the job has been completed. If you don't report back, the supervisor will have to find you to ask if the job is complete. A busy supervisor doesn't have time to track down every employee to see if they have completed their assigned tasks.

- **When you aren't sure how to proceed.** Situations may arise where you won't know how to complete a task. Whenever you don't know what to do, ask your supervisor. Remember the answer so you'll know how to handle a similar situation in the future.

- **When you have a problem.** Problems can always develop when you are trying to complete a task. The less experience you have, the more difficult it will be to solve the problem. Equipment may not work properly. Customers may have questions you can't answer. Someone else may not have done a job right and it keeps you from finishing your assignment. When you aren't sure how to solve the problem, contact your supervisor immediately. This will keep the problem from getting worse.

Some tasks may take you several hours, days, or weeks to finish. Keep your supervisor informed about on-going assignments. This shows you are assuming responsibility and your supervisor will come to trust you. It is important for supervisors to know they can rely on you to complete an assignment and keep them informed.

Taking Messages

There will be times when your supervisor won't be available to take phone calls. They might be out of the office or in a meeting. When this happens you will need to take a message for your supervisor. Here are some tips to remember when taking a message.

- **Tell the caller when your supervisor will return.** If you don't know, ask a co-worker for the information. If no one knows, inform the caller when you last saw your supervisor and assure them that their call will be returned as soon as possible.

- **Write down all the information.** Some organizations have electronic mail systems and send messages by computer. However, most organizations use message pads. These pads have specific areas for all the information already on them. If a pad like this isn't available, write down the following information:

1. Name of caller _____

2. Phone number _____

3. Message _____

4. Date and time of the call _____

5. Your name or initials _____

Always sign your name to messages you take so your supervisor can ask you questions about the message. If you have poor handwriting, print the message so it can be read.

- **Repeat the information back to the caller.** After you take down all of information, repeat the caller's name, phone number and message back to them. This ensures that all the information is correct.

- **Make sure your supervisor gets the message.** Put the message somewhere the supervisor is sure to see it, like a message box or desktop. Be sure to check back with your supervisor in case there are problems with the message. This shows you care about doing a job correctly. Sometimes it will be necessary to deliver urgent messages to your supervisor. Do so promptly.

Communicating About Job Performance

Your supervisor should communicate with you frequently about your job performance. This communication may be in the form of daily feedback about ways to improve your work, or on-the-job encouragement. It may sometimes be a negative experience. Here are a some simple guidelines to help you communicate effectively with your supervisor about job performance.

- **Don't respond to feedback with anger.** Feedback from your supervisor is important. Your supervisor should tell you about the things you have done right as well as the things you have done wrong. No one enjoys criticism, but it is sometimes necessary. If you get angry because your supervisor gives you negative feedback, get control of yourself before responding. Count to 10 if there is no other way to cool off. Sometimes your supervisor may yell at you. Do not get into a shouting match with your supervisor. Your supervisor should realize that there is no need for yelling and should then explain the situation in a rational manner.

- **Know what it is you have done wrong.** Your supervisor may be so upset with something you've done that you aren't sure what the problem is. Apologize if you made a mistake and ask for an explanation about exactly what you did wrong and the correct thing to do in the future.

- **Thank your supervisor for compliments.** You must learn to accept praise as well as criticism. Acknowledge compliments with a simple "thank you." You might say that you want to do the best job possible and appreciate knowing when you are doing it right.

- **Ask for feedback.** Some supervisors may not be good about giving feedback. If you aren't sure what your supervisor thinks about the work you are doing, ask! Let your supervisor know that you want to succeed on the job and need to know what they think.

Performance Appraisal

A performance appraisal is a periodic report about your job performance based on your supervisor's evaluation. You will be rated on various areas of your job. It could be a monthly, quarterly, or annual report depending on your organization's policy. Performance appraisals are not much different than a grading period in school. You will usually review the appraisal form with your supervisor and have an opportunity to respond to the evaluation. Some organizations give you the chance to rate yourself. You must then explain why you rated yourself that way. Be honest, but don't give yourself a rating lower than you deserve. New employees usually receive a performance appraisal during their probationary period.

Applying What You've Learned

Communicating with your supervisor is the most important thing you will do on the job. The following case studies will help you apply what you have learned in this section about communicating with your supervisor.

Case Study 1

Theresa has been working for Armstrong Dry Cleaners for two months. She works behind the counter taking customer orders. Her supervisor tells her the business is going to expand and begin cleaning leather garments. She tells Theresa that she will have to fill out a special order form for leather clothing. Theresa is not sure she understands all of the instructions.

1. What should Theresa do at this point?

   _____

   _____

   _____

Case Study 2

Bryan has just finished loading a truck when his supervisor comes up to him and starts yelling. He tells Bryan that a truck he loaded yesterday had several crushed boxes on it. The supervisor tells Bryan that he better get his act together if he expects to keep his job.

1. How should Bryan respond in this situation?

   _____

   _____

   _____

©1992, JIST Works, Inc. • Indianapolis, Indiana

Meeting a Supervisor's Expectations

It is important for you to do what your supervisor expects, which of course includes doing your job properly. We've already examined the significance of a job description in understanding your duties and discussed the importance of good, clear communication with your supervisor. Your supervisor expects you to communicate and should tell you what else is expected of you on the job. A supervisor may think their expectations are "common sense" and fail to communicate them to you. But these may not necessarily be common sense things. They may be things you learn the hard way from work experience. In this section we'll review some of the "little things" you need to know to get along with your supervisor. They are important because "little things" to you often become "big things" to your supervisor, as they are multiplied by all the workers they supervise.

There are six behaviors you should practice to satisfy your supervisor's expectations:

1. Being truthful
2. Being cooperative
3. Getting your work done

4. Being adaptive
5. Taking the initiative
6. Returning from your break on time

- **Be Truthful.** Your supervisor expects you to tell the truth at all times. If you make mistakes, don't try to cover them up by lying. Lies will usually be discovered and are grounds for dismissal. A supervisor needs employees they can count on to tell the truth at all times. Without honesty between the supervisor and workers, it is impossible for either to do a good job.

1. What are some reasons a worker might lie to their supervisor?

_____

_____

_____

_____

_____

2. What problems could be caused for the supervisor by these lies?

_____

_____

_____

_____

_____

_____

- **Don't Extend Your Breaks.** A supervisor expects you to work during your scheduled hours. Normally a full-time worker will be allowed a 15 minute break mid-morning and mid-afternoon in addition to a 30 minute or one hour lunch break. Your supervisor expects you to stay within the limits of your scheduled breaks. When you don't return from a break on time it can cause problems. A customer may have to wait, another worker may not be able to take their break, and others may not be able to finish a task until you complete your part of the job. If you can't get back from break on time, explain the reason to your supervisor. Make sure you aren't extending your breaks unless there is an exceptionally good reason.

  1. What are some acceptable reasons for extended breaks?

  _____

  _____

  _____

  _____

- **Get Your Work Done.** You should complete all assigned tasks as quickly as you can while doing the best job possible. Your supervisor will have difficulty checking your work all the time, but will expect you to continue working productively. If circumstances prevent you from completing a job, notify your supervisor immediately. You should balance your work between completing a task as quickly as possible and producing the highest quality of work you can. An inexperienced worker may have some difficulty understanding how to achieve this balance. Ask your supervisor for feedback about how well you are meeting these priorities.

  1. What obstacles might make it difficult or impossible for you to do your job?

  _____

  _____

  _____

  _____

- **Be Cooperative.** Cooperate when your supervisor asks for your assistance. When someone can't work a scheduled time, be willing to change your schedule if possible. Help with a task that is not normally your responsibility. In special situations your supervisor will need more help from everybody. Cooperation is a mutual thing and most supervisors will remember your help the next time you need a day off for a special reason. Thus, cooperation benefits you and also creates a more pleasant work atmosphere.

1. What are some reasons for cooperation?

_____

_____

_____

_____

_____

- **Be Adaptive.** Be willing to adapt to new situations. This means you are willing to change when necessary. The organization you work for will need to change as the world around it changes. Employees sometimes resist change because of poor self-esteem, threats to personal security, fear of the unknown, a lack of trust, or inability to see the larger picture.[2] When you understand the reason for resistance you can work to reduce it. You must be willing to adjust to change. Supervisors probably don't want to make changes any more than you do, but it is their responsibility to do so and they need your cooperation. It may help to think about all the positive things that will result from the changes.

  1. What are some typical reasons for change within an organization?

  _____

  _____

  _____

  _____

  _____

- **Take the Initiative.** You need to take the initiative to find ways to help your supervisor. There is probably always a lot of work to do. After your own work is completed look around your work site for other tasks to do. But it doesn't help anyone if your work suffers because you were trying to help with something else.

  1. How can you take the initiative to help your supervisor?

  _____

  _____

  _____

  _____

  _____

Applying What You've Learned

Remember the story of the explorer with the mosquito problem at the beginning of the book? Each example below contains some possible mosquitos or little things that a supervisor will notice. See if you can spot the "mosquito."

Case Study 1

Tonight Betsy has a date with Brad, the quarterback at Big Moose University. Marge, her supervisor at the Bureau of Motor Vehicles, is going directly from lunch to a supervisor's meeting. Betsy knows Marge won't be back in the office until 2:30 p.m. While on her lunch break, Betsy passes her favorite hair care center. A quick cut would make a great impression on Brad.

1. What is the mosquito?

   _____

   _____

   _____

2. What could the result be?

   _____

   _____

   _____

Case Study 2

Ryan has three days off this week. On his second day off, his supervisor, Peter calls. Ryan isn't home, but his sister takes a message. One of the other employees is sick and Peter needs Ryan to work the next day. Ryan was planning to visit his friend, Tyrone, at the state university.

1. What is the mosquito?

   _____

   _____

   _____

2. What could the result be?

   _____

   _____

   _____

Case Study 3

Leslie and Tanya come into the taco shop where Brandon works. It is almost closing time. The girls need a ride home. Brandon has finished nearly all the clean-up chores except sweeping out the back storage room. Leslie has to be home no later than 10:30 p.m., with no excuses accepted. She was grounded last week. It is 10:20 p.m. now.

1. What is the mosquito?

   _____

   _____

   _____

2. What could the result be?

   _____

   _____

   _____

Case Study 4

Adam has been working in the sporting goods section at the local department store for several months. Next week the store is having a big sale. Adam has been asked to help out in housewares during the sale. He likes golf clubs and baseball gloves, but isn't very fond of laundry baskets and blenders.

1. What is the mosquito?

   _____

   _____

   _____

2. What could the result be?

   _____

   _____

   _____

Case Study 5

Allie waits on customers at an ice cream parlor. It is mid-afternoon and the shop isn't busy. Two of Allie's friends stop by for a rest from some serious shopping. Leona, the store manager, is on her break. Allie's friends jokingly suggest that she provide them with a couple of "free" sample cones.

1. What is the mosquito?

   _____

   _____

   _____

2. What could the result be?

   _____

   _____

   _____

Resolving Problems with Your Supervisor

Each person looks at a particular situation from their own point of view. You will not always agree with your supervisor. Sometimes your supervisor may make a mistake. There may be times when you are not doing a good job. A number of situations may arise where a conflict will occur. Such disagreements may be resolved by conflict resolution, through a grievance procedure, or through disciplinary procedures.

Conflict Resolution

Conflicts are a part of life. Don't avoid conflicts when they arise. Talk with your supervisor about any disagreements. Below are some simple suggestions to help you keep conflicts to a minimum.

- **Don't accuse.** Everyone makes mistakes. When you make a mistake, you should do what you can to correct it. It's not a good idea to accuse your supervisor of making a mistake.

- **State your feelings.** Simply state your feelings about a situation. Don't say "you" when explaining your perception of the situation. It'll sound like you're accusing. Say "I feel," or "I think," or "I am" to describe your view. Your supervisor will not know how you feel unless you communicate.

- **Ask for feedback.** Ask your supervisor if you understand the situation correctly and have acted appropriately. It is possible you misunderstood what happened. You may find that once the situation is clarified you will feel differently about it.

- **State what you want.** Know what you want done about a situation before confronting your supervisor. State your wishes clearly and respectfully.

- **Get a commitment.** After you state your feelings and what you want done, find out what your supervisor can do about the situation. Maybe no action is necessary. If no immediate action can be taken, your supervisor should commit to a date and time to let you know what will be done.

- **Compromise when necessary.** Not all problems will be resolved the way you want. You may have failed to consider your supervisor's needs or the needs of the organization. How can your needs as well as your supervisor's be met? The ideal result of any conflict is that both parties are satisfied.

Most problems with your supervisor can be solved by these simple conflict resolution techniques. However, some problems can't be resolved in this manner. When such a situation occurs you may be able to file a grievance.

Grievance Procedures

If your supervisor is not able to resolve a conflict, you may get satisfaction going through a grievance procedure. Some organizations have standard procedures and you will need to check this out. Be aware that filing a grievance will almost always create stress between you and your supervisor.

Organizations with unions will have a procedure that has been negotiated between management and the union. If you are employed by such an organization, you will probably have a union representative with you at all steps in the grievance process. The final decision will then be made by an arbitrator.

Studies show about 62 percent of nonunion companies also have formal grievance procedures.[3] Many government or government-funded organizations are required by law to have grievance procedures. Some smaller organizations have no such process. You need to know your organization's procedure before filing a grievance. In nonunion organizations, you will have no assistance filing a grievance and the organization's personnel director or chief executive officer will probably make the final decision. Complaints of discrimination or sexual harassment often receive special attention. Such cases may require a different procedure.

You should make every attempt to resolve a conflict with your supervisor before filing a grievance. Don't tell your supervisor about the possibility of such action until you have tried every other means possible to solve the problem.

Disciplinary Action

There may be times when your work performance or behavior is unacceptable. It is your supervisor's responsibility to address the problem and advise you on appropriate performance. If you don't correct the problem, you could face disciplinary action. Make sure you understand your employer's disciplinary process. Such disciplinary procedures usually apply only to employees past their probationary period. Those still on probation may be dismissed without warning. Disciplinary procedures, like grievance procedures, vary from one employer to another. The action taken will depend on the seriousness of the violation. The four disciplinary steps explained on the next page are common to many organizations.[4]

1. **Oral warning.** Your supervisor warns you that your performance is not acceptable. This only applies to less serious problems. Serious problems such as drinking or drug use would probably result in immediate suspension or dismissal. The oral warning will probably go into your personnel record, and later be removed if no further problems arise.

2. **Written warning.** Repeated performance problems will result in a written warning. This step takes place after an oral warning is issued. A written warning may become a permanent part of your personnel record.

3. **Suspension.** Suspension means you won't be allowed to work for a short period of time, sometimes 3 to 5 days. This is unpaid time. This disciplinary action becomes a permanent part of the personnel record.

4. **Dismissal.** The final step of any disciplinary process is dismissal. This means the organization won't tolerate your job performance any longer. Dismissal becomes a permanent part of the personnel record. It also means that any future employer who contacts your former employer may be told that you were dismissed from your job.

Most organizations don't want you to fail. If you are being disciplined, follow your supervisor's instructions and you should not encounter further problems. Smaller businesses may not follow the procedure described above. You may simply get an oral warning before suspension or dismissal.

If you think you are going to be dismissed from a job, you may want to look for another job. You may also want to consider looking for another job when you can't resolve a problem with your supervisor.

Summary

Supervisors are individuals. Each one is unique. There are excellent supervisors and poor supervisors. This chapter has given you suggestions on how to get along with all types of supervisors. All supervisors appreciate good employees: they can't do their job without them. If you practice the guidelines in this chapter, you will increase your chances of establishing a positive relationship with your supervisor. If a problem does develop between you and your supervisor, try to resolve it. If a formal procedure is necessary, or your supervisor takes disciplinary action against you, make sure you understand how your organization handles such situations. Always try to abide by your employer's rules and guidelines.

Chapter Seven Endnotes

1. Thomas Von der Embse, *Supervision: Managerial Skills for a New Era*, (Macmillan Publishing Company, New York, 1987).

2. Barry Reece and Rhonda Brandt, *Effective Human Relations In Organizations*, (Houghton Mifflin Company, Boston, 1987), 353-354.

3. Anne Daughtrey and Betty Ricks, *Contemporary Supervision: Managing People and Technology*, (McGraw-Hill Company, New York, 1989), 541-543.

4. Von der Embse, op. cit.

Chapter Eight
Getting Along with Other Workers

TEAM CONCEPT

Teamwork is important in any business operation. Most managers and supervisors use team-building principles. A team is a group of people who work together to accomplish a common goal or an objective.

The use of the word team to refer to a work group is becoming increasingly common in modern organizations.[1] Teams are sometimes referred to as quality circles, self-managing teams, and work teams. Even if your organization does not use the word "team" to refer to the work group, managers and supervisors will expect you to work as part of a team. You should listen to instructions and cooperate with other employees to do the best job possible. That way everyone wins: you, the supervisor, the group and the organization.

Get to Know Your Co-workers

The terms "team" and "work group" are interchangeable in business and will be used the same way in this workbook. It is difficult to be a part of the team if you don't know how to get along with the other players. Getting to know your co-workers and being accepted by them will help you succeed in your job.

Listed below are several situations where you might interact with your co-workers. If you think the situation is appropriate and will help you get accepted by your co-workers, write "yes" in the space provided. If not, write "no."

_____Greet your co-workers when you arrive at work.

_____Join the office intramural sports league.

_____Ask a co-worker to join you for lunch.

_____Invite your co-workers to a party at your home.

_____Tell the group how much another worker spent on a new car.

_____Bring Aunt Sally's handmade rugs to sell to your co-workers.

_____Tell the latest ethnic joke during coffee break.

_____Loan a book you enjoyed to a fellow worker.

_____Offer to take on additional duties when a co-worker has to leave suddenly to tend to a sick child.

_____Repeat the latest rumor about the boss's relationship with a co-worker.

_____Tell the boss when one of your co-workers leaves early.

_____Tell the group how to do the job better.

_____Tell the group how well the boss thinks you are doing.

_____Offer to give a co-worker a ride to the auto repair shop.

How You Fit In

You need to know how you will fit into the team. This doesn't happen immediately. It will take some time before you know how to work well with the other employees in your work group. Everyone likes to be respected for their skills, knowledge or other contributions to the group productivity, but that respect won't come right away. If you do your job well, respect will increase as time goes by. Meanwhile, here are a few tips to help you begin to gain respect.

■ **Know your position.** Find out what other workers expect from you in addition to your supervisor's expectations. Other workers may have a specific method they use to do a job. If you do it differently, you may upset their whole system. Other workers might also expect the newcomer to take over certain tasks. For instance, cleaning up after a project or the end of the day. Go along with this. Eventually, another new worker will take over these tasks.

- **Accept good-natured teasing.** Other workers sometimes play jokes and tease a new worker to test what kind of person they are. If this happens, don't get angry. Let the others know you appreciate a good joke also. If this behavior doesn't soon cease and makes it difficult for you to do your work, you may want to talk to a co-worker about it before going to your supervisor. However, if you think the jokes or teasing is a form of discrimination or sexual harassment, let your supervisor know immediately.

- **Do your fair share.** Everyone in a work group is expected to do their best. If you don't do your fair share of the work, your co-workers will have to do more. After awhile, they may complain to the supervisor. The flip side is that the other workers might also complain if you do too much work because it could make them look bad. It's true that supervisors reward good workers with salary increases and promotions. But you should try to balance your work between both what the supervisor and co-workers expect. When in doubt, do what the supervisor expects.

- **Don't do other people's work.** As a member of a team you should cooperate and help others if asked. However, some people will try to take advantage of this cooperative spirit and push their work off on others. Beware. Your supervisor will evaluate you based on how well you do your job. If your job suffers because you are doing someone else's work, you will receive a lower evaluation. (Neither the person who takes advantage or the other workers will respect you more for this.)

- **Know how your team functions within the organization.** How does your team work with other teams in the organization? What are each team's responsibilities? Remember that all teams work to accomplish the employer's goals. Supervisors and managers should solve any team conflicts. Don't let conflicts affect your working relationships with members of other teams. You should all be working for the best interests of the organization.

Synergy

Synergy describes the extra energy and capability that results in combined group effort to accomplish an objective. It means that a team can accomplish more than the same number of people working individually. In this case:

$$1 + 1 = 3.$$

This is why teamwork is so important to an organization. You should cooperate in every effort to develop synergy between you and your co-workers.

Applying What You've Learned

Becoming part of the team is an important task for you to accomplish. Learning to be part of a work team is similar to becoming a part of other groups. Your work performance will be a major factor in getting accepted. The next two case studies are designed to help you learn how to become a team member.

Case Study 1

Rick began working in a warehouse a month ago. During the four weeks he has gotten to know a couple of the other workers pretty well. In fact, he went to a baseball game with Don last weekend. When he unwrapped his sandwich at lunch today there was no meat in it. Rick turned to the other workers and yelled that he was sick and tired of their jokes, then stomped out of the lunch room, slamming the door behind him.

1. How do you think the other workers will react to Rick's outburst?

   _____

   _____

   _____

2. What should Rick have done in this situation to create a more positive relationship with other workers?

   _____

   _____

   _____

Case Study 2

Lynette has worked at Hoover's Pharmacy for four days. Yesterday a customer broke a bottle of perfume. One of the other workers told Lynette to clean up the mess. She cleaned up the mess as she was told to do. Today, a small child knocked over a display of cough medicine. Another worker told Lynette to restack the boxes. Lynette got very upset and told the other worker to do it himself.

1. How do you think this will make the other workers feel about Lynette?

   _____

   _____

   _____

2. What do you think Lynette should have done in this situation?

   _____

   _____

   _____

The Value of Difference

Every person is unique. You will work with many people who are different from you. It is important for you to realize that differences are good. You should appreciate that all people are not like you. On a team, the strengths of one worker can overcome the weaknesses of another. The balance created by such variety makes a team stronger. There are three basic ways that people differ from one another. They differ in values, temperament, and individual diversity (gender, ethnicity, age, etc.).

Values

One major difference among workers is personal values. Values are the importance that we give to ideas, things, or people. The development of our values is influenced by parents, friends, teachers, religious and political leaders, significant events in our lives, and our community. While our values may be quite different, organizational behavior expert Stephen Robbins suggests that people fall into one of three general categories.[2]

1. **Traditionalist.** People in this category value:

   - Hard work
   - Doing things the way they've always been done
   - Loyalty to the organization
   - The authority of leaders

2. **Humanist.** People in this category value:

   - Quality of life
   - Autonomy (self-direction)
   - Loyalty to self
   - Leaders who are attentive to worker's needs

3. **Pragmatist.** People in this category value:

   - Success
   - Achievement
   - Loyalty to career
   - Leaders who reward people for hard work

What category do you fit into? Look over the values in each of the three categories. Circle those items that you value the most. Note which category has the most items circled.

1. Now, write down the category that you think best describes you personally. Explain your reasons.

_____

_____

_____

_____

_____

Effective Work Teams Blend Values

An effective work team is made up of people who have values in each category. At times the team needs the traditionalist to make sure that it does what is best for the organization. At other times, the team needs the humanist who stresses the need to balance life and work. There are also times that the team needs the pragmatist, who will strive to advance the team, because it also advances personal achievement. Each person's values are important to the team.

You may not fit neatly into just one category — many people don't. However, it helps us better understand and appreciate the differences with other people when we think about what category they might fall into. It is important to realize that you can't think in terms of right or wrong, good or bad, when you talk about value differences. Each set of values is sometimes positive and sometimes negative. Appreciate the differences and learn to be tolerant of people who hold a different set of values.

Temperaments

Your temperament is the distinctive way you think, feel, and react to the world. Everyone has their own individual temperament. However, experts have found it is easier to understand the differences in temperament by classifying people into four categories. There are many ways management specialists assess temperaments. One of the most famous is the Myers-Briggs Temperament Indicator. David Keirsey has adapted the Myers-Briggs and used it to identify four categories of temperament.[3] (I use Keirsey's description of the categories, but assigned different names to each category.)

1. **Optimist.** People with this temperament:
   - Must be free and not tied down
   - Are impulsive
   - Enjoy the immediate
   - Enjoy action for action's sake
   - Like working with things
   - Like to try new things
   - Can survive major setbacks
   - Are generous
   - Are cheerful

2. **Realist.** People with this temperament:
   - Like to belong to groups
   - Feel obligations strongly
   - Have a strong work ethic
   - Need order
   - Are realistic
   - Find tradition to be important
   - Are willing to do a job when asked
   - Are serious
   - Are committed to society's standards

3. **Pragmatist.** People with this temperament:
   - Like to control things
   - Want to be highly competent
   - Are the most self-critical of all temperaments
   - Strive for excellence
   - Judge people on their merits
   - Cause people to feel they don't measure up
   - Live for their work
   - Are highly creative
   - Tend to focus on the future

4. **Idealist.** People with this temperament:

- Are constantly in search of their "self"
- Want to know the meaning of things
- Value integrity
- Write fluently
- Are romantics

- Have difficulty placing limits on work
- Are highly personable
- Appreciate people
- Get along well with all temperaments

What kind of temperament do you have? Go through the descriptions above and circle the items in each style that apply to you. The category where you circle the most items is probably your temperament style.

1. Write down your temperament style.

_____

_____

How to Deal with Differences

There is no temperament style that is better than another. In fact, a team that includes people of all temperaments will be stronger. People with different temperament styles often find one another difficult to deal with because of their different approaches to life. When differences arise between yourself and a person of a different temperament, do the following things:

- Look for the positive contributions that person makes to the team.
- Identify the characteristics of your temperament that conflict with the other person's temperament.
- Talk with the person and explain what temperament characteristics seem to cause conflict between you.
- Ask the other person to describe which of your characteristics upsets them most.
- Develop a plan of how you can work together without conflict. Often just acknowledging the differences and being willing to discuss them will reduce the conflict.

Individual Diversity

The workforce has become more diverse over the past 20 years. This trend will continue throughout the 1990s. There are a number of ways the workforce differs. A study completed by the Hudson Institute for the Department of Labor called "Workforce 2000" describes these differences.[4]

1. **Gender.** Almost two-thirds of new workers entering the workforce before the year 2000 will be women.

2. **Ethnicity.** Twenty-nine percent of the new workers will be minorities. In addition, two-thirds of all legal immigrants (600,000 per year) will enter the workforce each year.

3. **Age.** The average age of workers will be 39 by the year 2000.

Individual diversity strengthens a team. Men and women often approach problems differently. Women are usually more attentive to the needs of other people while men tend to be more aggressive and ambitious.[5] Team members can learn from each other and build these positive characteristics into the work group.

People from different cultures and ethnic backgrounds look at problems from different points of view. Oriental cultures traditionally value cooperation, while western cultures emphasize individualism. People from different cultures can help one another develop a better appreciation of their values.

Age can also be a positive contribution. Younger workers usually bring enthusiasm and energy into a job. Older workers bring patience and their experience. These combined characteristics often make a team stronger.

No matter what the differences are, each person can contribute to the team. It is important for all the members of a team to share their thoughts and ideas. Understanding one another's viewpoint will help you overcome any differences.

Basic Human Relations

In this chapter, we examined why people differ and how you can work together. Below you will find some steps you can take to help you get along better with all the workers on your team.

Step 1. Get to know other workers. Take lunch breaks with the other employees. Join employee recreational and social activities. Listen to the things your co-workers share about their personal lives and interests.

Step 2. Don't try to change everything. You are the "new kid on the block" when you start a new job. Know and understand the organization before you think about changing something. Listen to others. Talk to co-workers about your ideas and get some feedback before you suggest changes.

Step 3. Be honest. One of the most important things you possess is a good reputation. Honesty with your co-workers will build up your reputation. It is one of the best ways to gain and keep their respect.

Step 4. Be direct. Let people know when they have done something that bothers you. Most people want to know when there is a problem, rather than have you be uncomfortable around them. Don't be a complainer or whiner. Make sure your problem is important before you take it to others.

Step 5. Avoid gossip. Don't listen to other people gossiping about co-workers. More importantly, never gossip about others. When you gossip, people wonder what you say about them and will avoid you.

Step 6. Be positive and supportive. Listen to the ideas of other people. When someone makes a mistake, don't criticize. It is irritating to have someone else point out a mistake. When you realize you've made a mistake, admit it and try to do better next time.

Step 7. Show appreciation. Be sure and thank a co-worker who does something to make your job easier. Let co-workers know that you appreciate their contributions to the team. People like to be recognized and praised.

Step 8. Share credit when it's deserved. Take credit for the work you do. When other co-workers assist you, make sure you credit them. People will feel they have been taken advantage of if someone else takes credit for their work.

Step 9. Return favors. A co-worker may help you out by exchanging a day off with you. Return that favor. A sure way to make people dislike you is to only take and never give.

Step 10. Live in the present. Avoid talking about the way things used to be. People don't want to hear about how great your old job was or how great former co-workers were.

Step 11. Ask for help and advice when it's needed. People like to feel needed. Your co-workers can be a great resource. When you aren't sure what to do, they can give you advice and assistance.

Step 12. Avoid "battles." Let co-workers with problems work out their own differences. Do not take sides in these situations. This is a sure way to develop problems with your co-workers. When you take sides, the other person will resent your interference.

Step 13. Follow group standards. Every group has standards. For example, they may take a coffee break at 9:15. Stop work and go on break with them if you are able. These group standards help build a team. Most standards are not major and require little effort to follow.

Step 14. Take interest in your co-worker's jobs. People like positive attention. Taking an interest in another worker's job will give that person positive attention. It also helps you better understand how your team works together.

Applying What You've Learned

Each person is a unique individual. Your co-workers will all have different ways of viewing life. In spite of these differences, you need to respect your co-workers. The way you react to differences could affect work relationships. Consider the following work situations and how you, as a co-worker, could react positively or negatively.

Case Study 1

Rosa's family has seven children and enjoys doing everything together. Her grandmother is celebrating her 85th birthday next Thursday. The family has planned a surprise party for her. On Monday when the work schedule is posted, Rosa finds out she is scheduled to work Thursday evening. She is very upset, though she knows she should have asked for that evening off before the schedule was made.

1. What could be your positive reaction to Rosa's problem?

   _____

   _____

   _____

2. What could be your negative reaction?

   _____

   _____

   _____

Case Study 2

Tyler belongs to an animal rights organizaiton. He brings literature about animal rights and leaves it in the break room. He refuses to eat meat because he believes killing animals for food is wrong. Tyler has invited you to join him at the next meeting of his favorite animal rights organization.

1. What could be your positive reaction to Tyler's invitation?

   _____

   _____

   _____

2. What could be your negative reaction?

   _____

   _____

   _____

Case Study 3

Don is a baseball fan. He has a season ticket to the hometown team's games. He collects baseball cards and brings them to work to trade with his co-workers' kids. He manages a little league team. During the World Series, Don brings his portable TV to work and watches the games during his breaks. From the time practice starts in March until the season ends in October, his conversation is about one subject — baseball.

1. What could be your positive reaction to Don?

_____

_____

_____

2. What could be your negative reaction?

_____

_____

_____

Case Study 4

Rochelle belongs to a religious group that doesn't celebrate any holidays. Next Tuesday afternoon, the boss is closing the office early. The entire staff is planning a big Christmas party for that day. Rochelle has asked to leave work early on the afternoon of the party.

1. What could be your positive reaction to Rochelle's request?

_____

_____

_____

2. What could be your negative reaction?

_____

_____

_____

Case Study 5

Gwen is a very hard worker. She comes to work early and stays late. She has to be reminded by her supervisor to take breaks. Her main interest is her job. Sometimes, she seems to be trying to outdo her co-workers.

1. What could be your positive reaction to Gwen's work habits?

    _____

    _____

    _____

2. What could be your negative reaction?

    _____

    _____

    _____

Case Study 6

Chang attends church on Saturday. He doesn't work on Saturdays because it is considered a holy day by his church. Last Saturday, all personnel were required to work due to a special project. Chang was excused from working Saturday. Your entire work group is upset with him.

1. What could be your positive reaction to Chang's situation?

    _____

    _____

    _____

2. What could be your negative reaction?

    _____

    _____

    _____

Special Problems with Co-Workers

Some problems that can occur on the job require special attention. They include sexual harassment, racial harassment, and dating. This section will review what you should know about each of these subjects.

Sexual Harassment

Sexual harassment is unwelcome verbal or physical conduct of a sexual nature. This can include such things as:

- Staring at another person
- Touching another person
- Telling sexual jokes
- Making sexual comments
- Commenting on a person's sexual characteristics
- Displaying nude pictures or obscene cartoons

Employers are required by law to protect employees from sexual harassment. You could be severely disciplined or fired for sexual harassment. You need to be very careful about doing any of the things listed above. Even if a person doesn't object to your behavior at the time, they can later say you intimidated them. It is better to be safe than sorry.

Racial Harassment

Racial harassment is unwelcome verbal or physical conduct of a racial nature. This might include such conduct as:

- Telling racial jokes
- Using racial slurs
- Commenting about a person's racial characteristics
- Distributing racial material
- Excluding someone from company activities because of race

This form of harassment is very unfortunate and usually results from ignorance. The previous section on valuing individual differences describes the importance of learning about people who are different from you. It is sometimes easy to participate in the bad behavior of other workers. When someone engages in racial harassment, point out the harm that can result. Don't participate in any of the behavior described above.

Dating

You get to know someone well when you work with them and may decide you would enjoy dating them. This is only natural. But dating a co-worker can be risky. For one thing, romantic advances might be considered sexual harassment. In fact, repeatedly asking someone for a date after being turned down could be considered sexual harassment.

Dating a co-worker can also have a negative effect on your relationships with other workers. They may feel that you take advantage of your romantic relationship. Perhaps they feel you are not doing all of your work. They may even feel you support that person's ideas or actions just because you are dating them.

Another problem that can result from dating a co-worker is that your attention is no longer on your job. You think about the other person when you are around them instead of concentrating on your work. You may want to talk with your date rather than work, or find yourself supporting your date's actions and ideas even when it may not be the right thing.

Another thing to think about is breaking up. What effect will breaking up have on your job performance and working relationship with the co-worker you dated? When you must work with that person everyday, you may experience a great deal of discomfort and stress.

Some organizations have a policy about dating co-workers. Be sure to find out if your employer has such a policy. If you do date a co-worker, be discreet. Don't talk about it in the office. Don't spend any more time with that person than is normally required. Try to separate how you behave toward the person at work and on a date.

Summary

Becoming part of the work team is important to your success on the job. Your relationship with other workers will affect your performance. Your contribution to the team will influence the way your supervisor appraises your job performance. Getting along with your co-workers is not difficult. It takes an understanding of yourself and an appreciation for differences between people. Finally, it takes a common sense approach to human relations. When all else fails, treat your co-workers as you would want to be treated. This doesn't mean treating them exactly like you would treat yourself. It does mean trying to understand how they want to be treated and then treating them accordingly.

Chapter Eight Endnotes

1. Tom Peters, *Thriving on Chaos*, (Alfred A. Knopf, New York, 1987).

2. Stephen Robbins, *Organizational Behavior: Concepts, Controversies, and Applications*, (Prentice Hall, Englewood Cliffs, N.J., 1989), 120.

3. David Keirsey and Marilyn Bates, *Please Understand Me: Character and Temperament Types*, (Prometheus Nemesis Books, Del Mar, Calif., 1978).

4. William B. Johnston and Arnold H. Packer, "Workforce 2000," (Hudson Institute, Indianapolis, 1987).

5. Judith Stevens-Long, *Adult Life: Developmental Process*, (Mayfield Publishing Company, Palo Alto, Calif., 1984), 215.

Chapter Nine

Problem-Solving Skills

PROBLEM-SOLVING SKILLS ARE IMPORTANT

Managing an organization today is complicated. There is competition from other countries. Technology is highly complex. Governemtn regulations are sometimes difficult to understand and know how to follow. Knowledge about how to run a business is increasing. Faced with this situation, employers are now looking for employees that can help solve problems created by these many complex factors.

Problem solving is a highly marketable skill. Employers are looking for people who can think on their feet. Learning to solve problems is important to your success on the job. In this chapter, you can practice seven steps to improving your problem solving skills.

Management Through Team Work and Employee Involvement

Managers in today's business world are relying on employees and work teams to help solve many problems. This is called employee involvement. Teams may be expected to solve any problems that occur. For example, if the data your team enters into a computer has a lot of mistakes, the team will be asked to solve the problem. There are several reasons employees are being asked to solve problems rather than just letting management solve them.

- **Reduction of Management.** The number of managers and supervisors is decreasing. This helps an organization save a great deal of money. It also means employees must assume some of the responsibilities previously performed by managers.

- **Complexity.** Modern business operation is very complex. World-wide competition, high technology, government regulations, and a diverse work force all make business more complex. An organization needs help from every employee to solve problems in these complex areas.

- **Motivation.** Employees are motivated to do a better job when they are involved in solving problems related to their work.

- **Proximity.** Employees are closer to most problems than managers and supervisors. They can often see solutions that escape managers.

- **Change.** Modern organizations go through a great deal of change. If employers want their employees to be more willing to change, they need to involve them in problem solving and decision-making processes.[1]

Employees who develop good problem-solving skills become valuable members of the team. They will be seen as good workers who should be rewarded with promotions and raises. This section examines skills you need to become a good problem solver.

Quality Circles

Experience has shown that the most effective way to manage workers is to involve them in the problem-solving process. Employees are more motivated when they have more control over their work. Participation in problem solving gives employees that control. Employee involvement is implemented through work teams. This process is sometimes referred to as employee participation. You may also hear the term "quality circle" used. A quality circle is a group of employees who meet in order to identify problems and find solutions.[2] The purpose of the quality circle is to improve the quality of services, products, and jobs.

Problem Solving

In order to be logical, problem solving should be a systematic process.[3] Some basic assumptions made about problems will help you understand this approach.

Basic Problem-Solving Assumptions

- **Problems can be solved.** It is important to believe a problem can be solved. This belief motivated some of the great problem solvers of history like Thomas Edison, inventor of the light bulb; Henry Ford, the creator of modern manufacturing processes, and Jonas Salk, who discovered the polio vaccine. These people persisted despite time and failures. Thomas Edison failed over 900 times before he produced a light bulb that worked.

- **There is a cause for everything that happens.** Problems have causes. Something makes the problem occur. You must look for the causes to solve the problem. Often, it is only possible to find probable causes.

- **Problem solving is a continuous process.** Any problem-solving system must be a continuous process. In other words, after finishing the last step in the process, we must return to the first step and begin the process again. This gives us the opportunity to evaluate whether the solution is working correctly or if it can be improved.

The Problem-Solving Process

The problem solving process can develop in a number of ways, but the steps and order you follow are important. Leaving out any of the steps or doing them in a different order will limit your problem-solving abilities.

Step 1. Identify the Problem. The biggest mistake you can make in solving a problem is to work on the wrong problem. Take time to discover what the real problem is. Here is an example of the importance of this step. A book store manager notices that the store is frequently out of certain titles. She defines the problem as "employees need to order books when they see that we have run out of a title." She then begins to work on getting employees to reorder books. However, the real problem could be something else. It could be that a standard number of books is ordered for each title when larger quantities should be ordered for more popular books. In this case, the problem should be defined as "how to improve inventory control."

Step 2. Gather and Organize Data About the Problem. You should gather as much data on the problem as possible. The best way to collect data is to observe what happens. Other good ways to collect data include talking with people involved and reading reports. Organize the data in a way that will help you arrive at a solution. This process is called analysis. Analysis requires some mathematical skills. There are three simple methods you can use to analyze your data: frequency tables, percentages, and graphs.[4]

Step 3. Develop Solutions to the Problem. After collecting data about the problem, you can begin to develop solutions. Develop as many solutions as possible in this step. There are several things you can do to develop solutions.

- **Talk to other people.** Talk the problem over with co-workers who have experienced the problem and find out how they solved it in the past. Ask friends from other organizations if they have had a similar problem and how they solved it. (When talking to others outside your organization, do not reveal information that would be considered confidential.)

- **Hold a group discussion.** The two most popular types of group discussion are:

  1. **Brainstorming.** Brainstorming sessions involve a group of workers trying to come up with as many ideas as possible. There are some important rules to follow when brainstorming. First, no ideas can be criticized. It is important to develop as many ideas as possible without being concerned about their quality. Second, stretch for ideas. When the group thinks that it has exhausted all ideas, try again to develop more ideas. Third, all ideas are written on flip charts and posted so that the entire group can see what's been suggested.

  2. **Nominal Group Technique.** This is a more controlled method than brainstorming. First, each person thinks of as many ideas as possible and writes them on a piece of paper. Second, the group shares these ideas, taking one idea from one person at a time. Third, the group discusses the ideas. Fourth, the group ranks or rates the ideas from best to worst.

- **Visit other organizations with similar problems.** You can learn a lot by discovering how other organizations solve their problems. Many businesses are willing to let you visit them if you don't work for a direct competitor. Look at their solutions and evaluate how well they have solved their problems. Decide if the solution could be used in your organization.

- **Read about the problem.** Trade journals provide valuable information about how organizations like yours have solved problems. Trade journals are magazines about a certain type of business. For example, there are trade journals for computer dealers, retailers, publishers, and fast food restauranteurs. The list goes on and on. Since trade journals deal with businesses just like yours, they publish articles that give helpful ideas about problems. Other business magazines or books may also give you some good ideas.

Step 4. Evaluate Possible Solutions. There are a number of questions you should ask when evaluating possible solutions.

- **Is the idea logical?** You should look for a relationship between the problem and solution. Make sure there is a direct relationship. For example, giving dissatisfied customers a discount doesn't solve the poor customer service problem.

—**How much will the idea cost?** You may have a great idea, but if it isn't affordable it doesn't do the organization any good. Some problems are not complicated; therefore, the solutions are not costly. However, costs for solutions to more complex problems can vary greatly. For example, pizza delivery time might improve if the store bought a new truck, but it may not be able to afford one.

—**Does the organization have workers who know how to implement the solution?** Some solutions require specialized knowledge. Without employees who have that knowledge the solution won't work.

—**Is the solution timely?** Some problems may need immediate solutions. Some ideas are good but take too long to implement. Sometimes it is necessary to choose two solutions; one that works immediately and another that will be a better solution for the future. For example, a new printing press will improve the quality of the company's printed documents, but delivery is three months away. The immediate solution then might be to reduce press speed, re-ink more often and have employees work overtime.

Even after applying these rules, it is difficult to select the right solution from a large number of ideas. Two ways to help sort ideas are rating and ranking.

1. **Rating.** Rating is a process where each idea is evaluated separately. You apply all four questions above to each idea. Then you rate it on a scale of 1 to 5, 1 being a very good idea and 5 a very poor idea. One drawback to this method is that you may end up with several ideas that are rated equal or almost equal.

2. **Ranking.** Ranking is another process. Look at all ideas, choose the best and rank it number one. Compare the remaining ideas and select the number two idea. Continue this process until all ideas have been ranked. A weakness of this method is that it is difficult to rank more than 10 ideas at a time.

Probably the best way to select the number one idea is to use both rating and ranking. First, rate all ideas. Then rank the top 10. This uses the strengths of each method and omits their weaknesses.

Step 5. Select the Best Solution. By the time you complete the analysis, you should be able to decide on the best solution. The best solution may not always be the top idea, but it will usually be among the top three to five ideas. Keep in mind these three things when choosing a solution:

- **The best idea may not be affordable.** This means that you should select an idea that will solve the problem without greatly increasing cost. If the top two or three ideas are basically equal, select the less costly one.

- **There's always risk involved.** No solution will be foolproof. This fact often keeps people from making a decision. You can try to reduce the risk, but you can't eliminate it.

- **Don't worry about being wrong.** Mistakes can't be totally eliminated. Think about what to do if the solution fails. Planning ahead for errors means they can be corrected more quickly.

Step 6. Implement the Solution. A good idea can be ruined if you fail to implement it correctly. Here are some guidelines to help you correctly implement ideas.

- **Believe in the idea.** Never implement an idea you don't think will solve a problem. Sometimes, if people believe an idea is successful it is easier to overcome difficulties that would otherwise jeopardize it.

- **Convince others to support the idea.** When a group solves the problem you already have this step implemented. It is extremely important to get the supervisor's support for any idea. A group solution will help convince your supervisor to support a solution. However, if you develop a solution by yourself, you need to convince other people to support your idea.

- **Don't let fear hold you back.** It is normal to be afraid of failure. Worries about losing your job or reputation if an idea fails need to be kept in check. People sometimes wait too long before implementing a solution. Inaction may cause a good idea to fail.

- **Follow through.** A solution shouldn't be immediately rejected because it doesn't work. It takes time for ideas to work. Continue trying the solution until you know why it isn't working before taking a new approach.

Step 7. Evaluate the Solution. Within a reasonable period of time, evaluate the effectiveness of the solution and decide if it is working. One good way to evaluate a solution is to repeat the analysis step. For example, go back and do another frequency table to find out if customers are happier, or if production or quality is improved, etc.

Creative Thinking

Many organizations realize that they must be innovative to compete with other businesses.[5] To do this employers want workers who think creatively. Creativity means the ability to think of new ideas. This may mean applying old ideas to new problems or coming up with entirely new ideas. Here are some suggestions to help you think creatively.

- **Don't let the problem limit your thinking.** Our thinking process sometimes limits the way we look at a problem. The following exercise illustrates blocks to creative thinking.

  —**Exercise 1.** Connect all nine dots with four straight lines without lifting your pencil off the paper. Look at the end of the chapter for the solution to this problem.

- **Look at the problem from different viewpoints.** Look at the problem in a variety of ways. Here is a simple way to help you do this. List ridiculous solutions to the problem. Then turn those ideas around and ask how they might make sense. This process is illustrated in the following example.

  Your supervisor has asked you and the other employees how to increase the number of customers who visit the shoe store where you work. Some ideas:

  - Give shoes away.
  - Yell at people to come into the store.
  - Have every style of shoe made.
  - Pay customers to take shoes.

  Making these ideas workable would give you the following:

  - Discount shoes as much as possible.
  - Get people's attention through advertising.
  - Have a wide variety of styles.
  - Include a free pair of socks with each purchase.

- **Use hazy thinking.** Other words for hazy are unclear or vague. Sometimes we're very specific and take things too literally in the problem-solving process. Maybe our thinking should be hazy and unclear. The next exercise illustrates how literal thinking can block creativity.

  —**Exercise 2.** Look at the letters below. Eliminate five letters to find one familiar word in the English language. After you've tried solving the problem, look at the answer at the end of this chapter. This exercise shows that thinking in such specific ways blinds us to alternative ideas.

  > F H I E V L E I L C E O T P T T E E R R S

- **Joke about the problem.** Humor is one good way that allows us to see the alternative solutions to a problem. Humor often relies on expectations. You are led to think one way, then surprised after seeing another way to look at a situation. This old riddle is an example. *Question:* What is black and white and read all over? *Answer:* A newspaper. When this joke is spoken "read" is usually interpreted as "red" because black and white lead a person to think about colors. Humor might allow you to view the problem in an entirely different way — an unexpected way.

- **Give yourself time to think.** Take time to think about the problem and solutions. Relax and look at the ideas that you've thought about.[6] Don't allow anything to distract you. Get away from phones, customers, co-workers, radios, televisions, and anything else that could keep you from just thinking about the problem and a solution. Write down your thoughts during this time or better yet, record them on tape so you're not distracted by writing. Then get away from the problem. Do something entertaining. Get together with friends. Relax. Often, this relaxation frees your unconscious to come up with more possible solutions.

There are other methods for being creative. Some of these ideas were already described in the problem-solving process, such as brainstorming and researching a problem. There are many excellent books on creative thinking. Find one and learn more about this valuable skill.

Summary

Problem solving is an important skill for employees in modern business. Many organizations expect every worker to contribute solutions to problems. You should practice your problem-solving skills whenever you get the chance. These skills will improve as you apply the techniques in this chapter.

Solutions to Creative Exercises

Exercise 1

Most people see that the dots make a square. They then think that you can't make your lines go outside this box. However, the instructions don't place this limit on you. You can't solve the problem unless you go outside the lines.

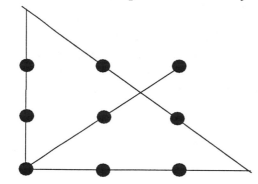

Exercise 2

You were to cross out five letters to find one familiar word. Most people will try to follow this instruction by crossing out 5 letters. However, the way to solve the problem is to cross out the words "five letters" like below.

F H I E N L E I L C E O A P A T E E R R S

Chapter Nine Endnotes

1. Rosabeth Kanter Moss, *The Change Masters,* (Simon & Schuster, Inc., New York, 1983), 180-205.

2. James Lau and A.B. Shani, *Behavior in Organizations: An Experiential Approach,* (Irwin, Homewood, Ill., 1988), 102-108.

3. Alfred Travers, *Supervision: Techniques and New Dimensions,* (Prentice Hall, Englewood Cliffs, N.J., 1988), 86.

4. LaVerne Ludden, *Instructor's Guide: Job Savvy—How to be a Success at Work,* (JIST Works, Inc., Indianapolis, 1992).

5. William Miller, *The Creative Edge: Fostering Innovation Where You Work,* (Addison-Wesley Publishing Company, Inc., Reading, Mass., 1987), 230.

6. James Adams, *The Care and Feeding of Ideas,* (Addison-Wesley Publishing Company, Inc., Reading, Mass., 1986), 123-124.

Chapter Ten

Ethics: Doing the Right Thing

WHAT ARE ETHICS?

Ethics are principles or standards that govern our behavior. Ethical principles are usually set by society. Our communities, organizations, religions and families establish ethical principles that guide us in our daily actions. In this chapter, we will examine ethical behavior on the job. This is what should govern the way you behave toward your employer, supervisor, co-workers and customers. As we begin, let's look at how you view ethical behavior.

What Is Ethical Behavior?

At first glance, ethical behavior seems easy. All you've got to do is the right thing. Knowing what is the right thing for every situation is the difficult part. Also, what you consider "right" or "ethical" may differ from others. Most people learn ethical behavior while growing up and use the same principles as adults.

1. List below the reasons you feel ethical behavior is important.

_____

_____

_____

2. List common ethical behaviors observed by most people.

_____

_____

_____

3. Now list some job situations where you would need to apply ethical principles.

_____

_____

_____

Ethical Decision-Making Problems

Sometimes it is difficult to know what is the right behavior. There are three basic problems that most people have when trying to decide the right thing to do.

1. **Not knowing what is expected.** There are times you may face a situation and not know what is right or wrong. Perhaps you've never been in that situation before, or been confronted with those same circumstances.

   - For example, you deliver a package and the customer offers you a tip. You're a new employee and don't know if the company allows you to accept tips. You also don't know if you're supposed to report any tips.

     1. What would you do in this situation?

     _____

     _____

     _____

     _____

2. Conflicts in ethical standards. A major problem can result when your ethical standards conflict with those of others. This type of conflict can occur between you and your co-workers, supervisor, or organization.

- There may be conflicts between your ethics and those of co-workers. For example, you and two other workers are out on a repair job for a telephone company. They decide to report that the repair job will take 3 hours, when in fact it will only take 2 hours. They plan to spend the extra hour drinking in a bar.

  1. What would you do in this situation?

  _____

  _____

  _____

  _____

- You may have ethics conflicts with your supervisor. For example, you work for a painting contractor. At the end of a day's work, your supervisor tells you to take some partially empty paint, varnish, and turpentine cans to the county landfill. You know that it is illegal to dispose of these materials in a landfill.

  1. What would you do?

  _____

  _____

  _____

  _____

- Your ethics may conflict with those of the organization's. This can happen when a company supports policies that you believe are wrong. For example, you work for a restaurant that regularly substitutes a lower grade of meat than is advertised on the menu.

  1. What would you do in this situation?

  _____

  _____

  _____

  _____

3. **Dilemmas about a situation.** Not every ethical decision is strictly right or wrong; pure black or white. In these situations it can be very difficult to decide how to behave.

■ For instance, you are a bank teller. A co-worker confides that he is working on a GED. You know that a high school diploma or GED is one of the bank's hiring requirements. It is obvious that the co-worker lied on his application. In the entire time you have known him, he has always done an excellent job as a teller. You know that he has a wife and two children who depend on his income from this job. You question whether you should report this information to your supervisor.

1. What would you do?

_____

_____

_____

_____

Guidelines for Making Ethical Decisions

The problems illustrated above show the difficulty in making ethical decisions. Did you have trouble trying to decide how you would act in the situations described? Most people would have some difficulty. However, there are some questions you can ask yourself when making ethical decisions. These questions can help guide your behavior. You may need to answer several or all of the questions before you can make the right decision. Just because you can answer one question doesn't mean the act you are considering is ethical.

1. **Is it legal?** This refers to local, state, and federal laws. Laws express the ethical behavior expected of everyone in society. You should consider if you could be arrested, convicted, and punished for your behavior.[1] In the example about disposing paint cans in a landfill, it is clear that doing what the supervisor wanted would be illegal. When you do something illegal, your behavior will not be excused simply because you were ordered to do it.

2. **How will it make you feel about yourself?** It is important to consider how you will feel about yourself if you behave in a certain way. A good self-concept is one key to doing right. A book co-authored by Norman Vincent Peale and Ken Blanchard states: "...people who have a healthy amount of self-esteem tend to have the strength to do what they know is right—even when there are strong pressures to do otherwise."[2] What you're really asking is: Am I at my best? Most of us want to do our very best. We want to look at ourselves in the mirror without feeling guilt.

3. **How do others feel about it?** You should discuss ethical problems with others. It may be difficult to share the problem with your supervisor. Talk with a co-worker you trust. You can also talk to friends, relatives, religious leaders, or anyone whose opinion you respect. Don't just talk to people you think will agree with you.[3] Listen to advice from others, but don't assume the majority is always right.

4. **How would you feel if the whole world knew about it?** You might think of this as the "60 Minutes" test. What if a TV reporter from "60 Minutes" showed up to broadcast what you are doing? When you don't want co-workers, supervisors, friends, relatives, or the community to know what you are going to do, then don't do it.

5. **Does the behavior make sense?** Is it obvious that someone could be harmed? Understand that you might harm someone physically, mentally or financially. Is it obvious that you will get caught? This last question shouldn't be the only thing you consider, but you should keep it in mind.

6. **Is the situation fair to everyone involved?** Ethical behavior should ensure that everyone's best interests are protected.[4] Look at how everyone can benefit, but realize that everyone will not benefit equally by the decision you make. However, no one should receive a great gain at the expense of someone else. If someone is clearly disadvantaged, they might look for ways to "even the score."

7. **Will the people in authority at your organization approve?** How does your supervisor feel about the behavior? What would the manager of your department say? Would it be approved by the organization's lawyer? Find out what those in authority think about the situation. This does not guarantee the right decision. It is possible for people in authority to support unethical behavior. You aren't necessarily relieved of responsibility because a supervisor approves a certain act.[5] However, asking for approval indicates what behavior is thought to be right by people in authority at your organization.

8. **How would you feel if someone did the same thing to you?** This is also the "Golden Rule" or "do to others what you would want them to do to you." When applying this principle, you should look at the situation from another person's point of view. Avoid doing things you think would be unfair to you, because it is also probably unfair to someone else.

9. **Will something bad happen if you don't make a decision?** There could be times when you decide to do nothing and it won't affect anyone. You may have good reasons for not wanting to get involved. However, you may be aware of a situation that could result in someone being hurt. Not taking action when you think you should can result in a major problem. The other option is to give an example when it would be acceptable not to make a decision.

It is important to ask as many of these questions as you can when trying to make an ethical decision. Asking only one question is not likely to result in the best ethical choice. The more principles you can apply, the better your ethical choice will be.

Applying What You've Learned

Review the ethical problems described below. Apply the ethical questions above to these problems and decide what you would do.

Case Study 1

Roger works for the license branch. He saw one of the driving examiners take a bribe from an elderly woman. Roger knows the woman. She lives alone and needs to drive her car to get groceries and do other business. He has never seen the examiner take a bribe before.

1. What do you think Roger should do? Explain your answer.

_____

_____

_____

_____

Case Study 2

Lisa works for a screw and bolt manufacturer. The company has a contract with the Air Force. Lisa knows that the bolts being made for the Air Force are not up to the required standards. She talked with her supervisor and he said not to worry about it. He said it was up to management to correct the problem.

1. If you were Lisa, what would you do? Explain your answer.

_____

_____

_____

_____

Case Study 3

Jane works in a jewelry store. A customer left two rings for cleaning, but Jane accidentally gave her a receipt for just one ring. The customer didn't notice the mistake and left the store before Jane realized what she had done. One of the rings is quite beautiful. Jane thought about how nice it would look on her. She began to think about keeping the ring for herself and telling the manager the customer left only one ring. After all, the customer was very wealthy and could afford the loss.

1. What do you think Jane should do? Explain your answer.

_____

_____

_____

_____

Go back to the situations presented earlier in the chapter. Apply the ethical questions to these situations. What would you do differently if anything? Explain your reasons for each situation.

1. Taking a tip from a customer.

   _____

   _____

   _____

   _____

2. Taking an extra hour with the repair crew.

   _____

   _____

   _____

   _____

3. Dumping paint cans in the landfill.

   _____

   _____

   _____

   _____

4. Substituting lower grade meat.

   _____

   _____

   _____

   _____

5. Reporting a worker who lied on his application.

   _____

   _____

   _____

   _____

Common Ethical Problems

There are some common ethical problems that workers often face on the job. Listed below are seven areas where knowing how to behave can keep a new worker out of trouble.

1. **Favoring friends or relatives.** This is a particular problem in a business that deals directly with the public. Many businesses allow employee discounts for immediate family members (father, mother, spouse, brothers and sisters). However, friends may expect special deals and service. As a result, paying customers do not get proper service because of the attention shown to friends. Know what your employer permits and expects in these situations.

   ■ List some ways that workers could show favored treatment to friends and relatives.

   _____

   _____

   _____

2. **Cheating the employer out of time**. An employer pays employees for time spent at work. Some workers cheat the employer out of this time in a number of ways such as:

   ■ Breaking for longer periods than is allowed.

   ■ Talking excessively with friends and relatives while at work.

   ■ Coming to work late or leaving early.

   ■ Hiding someplace to avoid working.

   ■ Conducting personal business using office equipment.

   This type of behavior is very irritating to supervisors. Less work gets done and customers may not be satisfied. When employees behave this way, disciplinary action may be taken.

   ■ List some other ways workers can cheat employers out of time.

   _____

   _____

   _____

3. **Stealing from the company.** Taking money from the cash register or taking merchandise from a store are obvious ways of stealing. However, there are three things workers often steal without realizing it.

   ■ **Supplies.** People take pens, pencils, paper, paper clips and other supplies from their employer. It doesn't seem like a big thing because the organization has so many supplies. However, multiplied by all employees it can cost an organization a great deal of money.

- **Photo copies.** Many employees use the copy machine for personal use without thinking of it as theft. However, it usually costs a business about 2 to 5 cents per copy. Making 20 copies may cost $1. If every employee in an organization with 1,000 employees did this once a week it would cost the employer almost $52,000 a year. Small thefts by workers can add up to major expenses for an organization.

- **Long distance phone calls.** This is one of the most expensive crimes in an organization. Telephone companies charge more during business hours. Making personal long distance calls on the organization's phone system can add up to lots of money. Some employees think this is okay when the company has WATS lines (Wide Area Telephone Service). WATS lines are not free. The organization gets reduced rates for purchasing a certain amount of long distance phone line time.

- What are other ways employees steal from their employers?

  _____

  _____

  _____

4. **Abusing drugs and alcohol.** Drinking alcoholic beverages or using drugs on the job is wrong. Taking "recreational" drugs or nonprescription drugs is against the law. Using them on the job can result in immediate termination. Three major job problems related to substance abuse are:

   - **Lower productivity.** Employees produce less goods or services. But because of their altered state of mind, they may think they are producing more.

   - **Lower quality.** It is impossible to perform at your best when under the influence of alcohol or illegal drugs. The quality of work will be less than your employer is paying you to provide.

   - **Safety hazards.** Substance abuse can cause many safety problems. Since reactions are slowed, workers are more likely to suffer serious or fatal injuries.

   - List other problems created by substance abuse on the job.

     _____

     _____

     _____

5. **Violating matters of confidentiality.** Some employees have access to a great deal of information. If you are in a position to handle such information, don't talk to anyone about it. This especially includes other workers. Confidential information may include:

- **Company finances.** This is information about company earnings, profit, wages and salaries, and payments to suppliers. This information must be kept private for businesses to compete with one another. Sharing information about wages and salaries can cause embarrassment and hard feelings between workers. Most workers will get upset if this information is shared.

- **Customers.** This could include very private information, such as credit history or criminal records. Less critical information like the amount of money spent with your organization could still cause harm to someone.

- **Employees.** This may include personnel records, performance appraisals, or attendance records. Talking about any of this information with others could harm the employee's reputation or bring about other problems.

Many companies have policies about confidentiality. You should know your employer's policies. However, it is in everyone's best interest for you to keep all information confidential.

- List other information that should be treated as confidential.

_____

_____

_____

_____

6. **Knowing about other employees' unethical behaviors.** One of the most difficult situations to face is knowing that another employee has done something wrong. There are two reliable ways of finding out about this type of situation:

   1. The other employee may tell you personally, or

   2. You see the employee do something wrong. If this happens, you should feel some obligation to report the problem to your supervisor.

Gossip is another way of finding out about another employee's misdeeds. Do not feel obligated to report what you hear to a supervisor. In fact, when you don't have firsthand information about a situation, it is better not to repeat what you've heard to anyone.

- List some things you may discover about other workers that might need to be reported to your supervisor.

_____

_____

_____

_____

7. **Violating the organization's policies.** Many organizations develop a set of personnel policies to govern employee behavior. Policies are communicated through a policy manual or in the form of memos. As an employee, you are expected to follow these policies. You can be disciplined for violating policy. It is important to know what the policies are and to follow them. Even if other workers get away with breaking the policies, you should not accept this as a good reason for breaking them yourself.

- List some common personnel policies an organization might have established.

  _____

  _____

  _____

  _____

How you deal with ethical problems like those discussed above is very important to your job success. The wrong behavior could cause your supervisor to be very dissatisfied with your performance and could, in fact, cause you to be fired from your job.

Applying What You've Learned

Look over the following cases and apply what you've learned about ethics to each of the situations described.

Case Study 1

Shane works in the payroll department. He has several friends in the computer department. One of these friends, Fran, told him that she just got a raise. Her supervisor told her that she is now the most highly paid programmer in the company. Shane knows there are several other programmers that have a higher salary than Fran has been promised. The supervisor has obviously lied to Fran.

1. Should Shane tell Fran what he knows? Explain your answer.

   _____

   _____

   _____

   _____

Case Study 2

Justine works in a donut shop. Some of her friends stop by late at night. She spends a lot of time talking with them, but there aren't any customers in the shop. A customer comes in and Justine immediately asks if she can help him. She then returns to her friends' table and starts talking with them.

1. Do you think Justine is doing the right thing by spending so much time talking with her friends? Explain your answer.

_____

_____

_____

_____

Case Study 3

Lance works for a fast food restaurant. He comes from a very poor family. The restaurant has a policy of throwing out any hot sandwiches that aren't sold within 15 minutes. The policy also states that employees are not to take any of the sandwiches for themselves. Lance is told by his supervisor to throw away about 10 cheeseburgers. He thinks about how much his family could use the sandwiches. Instead of throwing them in the dumpster, he hides them in the back of the store and takes them home when he leaves work.

1. Should Lance have done this? Explain your answer.

_____

_____

_____

_____

Summary

Managers and supervisors will evaluate you based on your behavior. If they see you do something they consider unethical, you may be disciplined. To maintain a good self-concept, you need to behave in a way that you feel is ethical. The problem is that it is not always easy to know what is ethical. If you apply the questions suggested in this chapter, it will help you make the best decision when you face ethical problems.

Chapter Ten Endnotes

1. Thomas Garrett and Richard Klonoski, *Business Ethics*, (Prentice Hall, Inc., Englewood Cliffs, N.J., 1986), 9.

2. Kenneth Blanchard and Norman Vincent Peale, *The Power of Ethical Management*, (William Morrow and Company, Inc., New York, 1988), 47.

3. Archie Carroll, Business and Society: *Ethics & Stakeholder Management*, (South-Western Publishing Co., Cincinnati, 1989), 117.

4. Larue Hosmer, *The Ethics of Management*, (Irwin, Homewood, Ill., 1987), 100-103.

5. Manuel Valasquez, *Business Ethics: Concepts and Cases*, 1988, 42-43.

©1992, JIST Works, Inc. • Indianapolis, Indiana

Chapter Eleven

Getting Ahead on the Job

WHAT CONCERNS A NEW WORKER

Two issues that usually concern new workers after being on the job for a few months are pay increases and promotions. These are common conerns. There are no standard answers, because each organization is different. Let's examine a few points about each of these issues.

Getting a Raise

There are many general reasons organizations give pay raises.[1] Good pay helps organizations attract and keep good people. Raises are one way to reward good performance. The thought of more money can help motivate employees to do a better job. But it is important to know when it is reasonable to expect a raise. Unreasonable expectations can create misunderstandings between you and your employer. This in turn may cause you to lose interest in your job.

An organization's policy on pay increases is usually discussed during the job interview. If it hasn't already been explained to you, ask your supervisor to tell you how pay raises are determined. Below are some common instances when employers give pay increases.

- **Completion of Probation.** Probation can last from one to six months. Organizations usually give raises after a new employee has completed the probation period. Probation is considered a training period. After completing training, a new worker has demonstrated the ability to do the work expected by the organization.

- **Incentive Increases.** Organizations that use this method pay for raises according to the quality of work during a certain time period. Typically the work is evaluated every six months or once a year. Pay increases are based on evaluations and job performance. Organizations stressing teamwork might give pay increases based on the team's evaluation.

- **Cost of Living Increases.** This type of increase is sometimes given to help employees offset inflation. Inflation is the increase in prices that lowers the value of the dollar. For example, if inflation rises 6 percent a year, at the end of that year $1 is only worth 94 cents. In this situation, an employer might give employees a 6 percent cost of living increase so the buying power of their pay doesn't decrease.

- **Keep Employees.** Organizations may give highly valued workers pay increases to keep them from taking other jobs. If you receive a higher paying job offer, it is appropriate to ask your employer for a raise. Don't use this approach unless you really have a better offer you're considering. In addition to damaging your credibility, your employer may not be able to afford a raise and tell you to take the other job.

- **Reward for Special Efforts.** Sometimes employees take on added job responsibilities. Employers may reward this by giving raises. Some organizations reward employees for learning new skills. The more skills you learn, the more money you earn.

- **New Assignments.** Raises are normally given along with new positions in the same organization, especially if it means a promotion to a more responsible position. Some businesses give increases based on the number of jobs a worker learns to do. The more jobs you are trained to do, the higher your pay.

When you start a new job it is important to understand your employer's policy on pay increases. You are less likely to be disappointed by the size of your pay raises if you know what to expect. Knowing how your employer gives pay raises gives you an advantage and the motivation to work hard to receive a raise.

The Difference Between Wage and Salary

A wage is a specific amount of money earned for each hour worked. A salary is a flat payment per week or month regardless of hours worked. Employers are required by federal law to pay hourly workers an overtime rate for hours worked in excess of 40 hours per week. Salaried workers are usually more highly paid because they don't receive overtime pay. It is possible for salaried workers to make less than hourly workers in the same organization if the hourly workers are working a lot of overtime.

Appyling What You've Learned

Read the following situations and answer the questions that follow each case.

Case Study 1

Keith works as a grill cook for Humpty Dumpty Hamburgers. He was told he would receive a raise after working for the store for three months and could be considered for another raise after six months at his job. Keith has worked at the store for six months and still hasn't received a raise. Keith's supervisor has never talked with him about his job performance.

1. Do you think Keith deserves a raise? Explain the reason for your answer.

   _____

   _____

   _____

2. What approach should Keith take when asking for a raise?

   _____

   _____

   _____

Case Study 2

Roberta has worked as a clerk for Golden Auto Parts for more than three years. Each year she received a 5 percent raise. During the past year, inflation was 6 percent. Roberta does a good job and her supervisor frequently praises her for her work. She is concerned that if she receives the same pay increase as in past years, it will not be enough money for her to live on.

1. What is the percent of pay increase you think Roberta should ask for?

    _____

    _____

    _____

2. How did you decide on the percentage?

    _____

    _____

    _____

3. What approach do you think Roberta should follow when discussing her raise?

    _____

    _____

    _____

Case Study 3

Barb has worked as a secretary for the Newton Manufacturing Corporation for two years. Her performance appraisals have always been good and she has received a good pay raise each year she's been with the company. Recently, Barb saw a want ad in the newspaper for a secretary. The advertised pay was $1,000 more per year than she is currently making. Barb believes she has the qualifications needed for the advertised job, and becomes upset that she isn't being paid more by Newton. She plans to go into the office on Monday and tell her supervisor that she could have a job that would pay her $1,000 more than she is making at Newton.

1. Do you think Barb's plan is a good one? Explain the reason for your answer?

    _____

    _____

    _____

2. What plan would you suggest?

    _____

    _____

    _____

Case Study 4

Wayne is a bookkeeper for Hall's Home Oil Company. A few months ago his supervisor asked him to set up all the ledgers on a new computer system the company purchased. The new system has many advantages. The managers now receive financial reports that help save the company several thousand dollars each month. Wayne works hard to keep the computer system functional. He has begun to wonder why he has been given this new responsibility, but no pay raise.

1. Do you think Wayne deserves a raise? Explain the reason for your answer.

   _____

   _____

   _____

2. What plan would you devise for Wayne to get a raise?

   _____

   _____

   _____

Getting Promoted

Not everyone wants a more responsible position, but many people do. Promotions have several advantages. These advantages include:

- **Increased Pay.** Normally, pay raises accompany promotions. However, sometimes a promotion to a salaried position is not much more money than an hourly worker earning overtime pay.

- **More Respect.** Co-workers and people outside the organization will pay you more respect. A promotion increases your status.

- **Better Assignments.** You will do work that is more challenging to you. Lower level positions usually require less ability and sometimes workers become bored in these jobs.

- **Improved Self-Esteem.** Your own self-esteem will improve when other people recognize you and your work. You'll feel better about yourself because of your success.

Promotions are normally based on two major criteria — seniority and merit.[2] Seniority refers to the amount of time on the job. Workers with more seniority often understand the organization and job better. Merit refers to the quality of job performance. Both merit and seniority are considered when deciding which employee to promote. If specific skills or knowledge are required for the job, that is also a factor. If you want to be promoted, follow these tips:

- **Keep Track of Job Openings.** When a job vacancy occurs, apply for the job. Talk to other workers. They usually know when someone is going to retire, get a promotion or leave for another job. Some companies "post" job openings. Posting is a system for notifying employees of vacancies by placing notices on a bulletin board, in the company newsletter, through memos or some other means.

- **Talk to Your Supervisor.** Tell your supervisor you are interested in a promotion. Supervisors should know where the vacancies are in the company. If you have a good work history your supervisor should also be willing to give you a good recommendation.

- **Notify the Human Resources Department.** You should let the Human Resources (personnel) Department know you want a promotion. They will ask your supervisor about your job performance and keep you in mind when openings occur. In some organizations it is appropriate to notify your supervisor first. Find out the proper process for your organization.

- **Create a Network.** Networking refers to building friendships with co-workers in other departments. Secretaries are excellent people to include in your network because they have access to a great deal of information. Ask people in your network to notify you when they hear of possible job openings. For a network to work well, you must be willing to share information and help others in your network. People in a network should be willing to share information with each other.

- **Develop a Good Reputation.** Be a dependable and reliable employee and work hard. Get along with your co-workers. Become highly skilled in your job assignment. When you do these things supervisors and managers will notice and remember you when a promotional opportunity arises.

- **Create Your Own Job.** It is possible to create a job for your own promotion. Look for ways to improve your organization. Make suggestions to accomplish these improvements. It is natural for management to reward your creative thinking by placing you in a new job to carry out your suggestions.

When Promotions Occur

Promotions only occur when your organization has a job vacancy or the money to create a new job. You need to be patient about getting a promotion. However, when someone with less seniority than you receives a promotion, you should ask why. Discuss with your supervisor the difference between you and the other worker. Ask for suggestions to improve your performance. Take your supervisor's advice. It will help you better compete for the next promotion.

1. List the skills you think a worker needs in order to get a promotion. (Note: Think about everything this workbook taught you about being a successful employee.)

_____   _____

_____   _____

_____   _____

_____   _____

Applying What You've Learned

Read the following cases and decide which employee to promote. Refer to the list of work skills you just completed if you have trouble making a decision.

Case Study 1

Lou has been a carpet layer at the Carpet Emporium for two years. He is dependable and gets along well with the other workers. He is very creative and often suggests time-saving methods of carpeting homes. Lou often criticizes and argues with the supervisor, but always gets the job done.

Jan has worked at the Emporium for 16 months as a carpet layer. He is also dependable and gets along well with the other workers. Jan took some supervising classes at the local community college. He goes out of his way to help the supervisor and gets along well with him.

Business at the Carpet Emporium has been very good. Management has decided to form an additional work crew to lay carpet. The department manager can't decide whether to promote Lou or Jan to supervise the new crew.

1. Who would you promote to the new supervisor's position?

_____

_____

_____

2. Explain the reasons for your selection.

_____

_____

_____

Case Study 2

Jerry has been a secretary at Happy Acres Real Estate Agency for over two years and is currently taking a real estate course at the local junior college. He will complete the course in time to take the real estate license test next month. He learned through the office grapevine that one of the agents plans to retire within three months. Jerry talked to the manager about a promotion to an agent's position.

Bobbi came to work for the agency six months ago. She has a realtor's license, but because the agency wasn't hiring any more agents at that time, she took a position administering the deeds and titles in the office.

Jerry's information is correct. The agency is looking for another agent to replace the one who is retiring. The agency manager plans to promote from within the company, rather than hiring someone new. Jerry and Bobbi are the candidates.

1. Who would you promote to the agent's position?

   _____

   _____

   _____

2. Why did you choose to promote this person?

   _____

   _____

   _____

Case Study 3

For the past two years, Marion has worked part-time for the Golden Years Home, a residential health care center. Marion first started working in the home as a volunteer when she was a junior high school student. During high school, she worked as a kitchen aide. Marion is studying to be a licensed practical nurse while continuing to work weekends at the health care center. The staff knows they can depend on Marion to be flexible. She has recently expressed an interest in working full-time.

Terry has been a volunteer at the home for two years and is a recent high school graduate. After graduation, she applied for a full-time position at the home and was hired as a nurse's aide. As a volunteer, Terry worked with the activities director during social times for the residents and helped plan many social events. Last summer, Terry traveled with the group to the Senior Citizen's Olympics held in the state capital. The residents consider Terry "an adopted grandchild."

Because of an increase in the number of residents, the health care administrator decided to create a new stafff position — assistant activities director. Both Marion and Terry are being considered for the position.

1. Who would you promote or hire for this position?

   _____

   _____

   _____

2. Why did you choose this person?

   _____

   _____

   _____

Case Study 4

Charlene has been a waitress at the French restaurant, "Monsieur Jacques" for one year. Charlene is known for excellent service. Customers often ask to be seated at Charlene's tables. She receives very good tips because of her speeed in serving. She is impatient with the kitchen workers and those bussing tables when their work slows down her service. Charlene likes to work the business lunch crowd and usually refuses to work at other times. She knows many of the lunch customers by name and greets them as they are seated.

Alex has worked at "Monsieur Jacques" for two years. He is dependable and serves customers satisfactorily. Alex rarely visits with the customers, but is always polite. He gets along well with co-workers and is willing to adjust to new work hours when needed. He even helps clear tables during rush hour. Last week the chef shared his "secret" crepe recipe with Alex. No one in the restaurant has known the chef to do this before.

Due to an increase in business, the restaurant manager has decided to add a "maitre de" during lunch hour. This person would be responsible for greeting and seating customers, as well as honoring reservations. Charlene and Alex are both being considered for the promotion.

1. Who would you choose as the "maitre de?"

   _____

   _____

   _____

2. Why did you choose this person?

   _____

   _____

   _____

Career Development

The term career development refers to the process of reaching your personal goals in work and in life. Career development may not seem important during the first few years of your work experience. However, it is important to understand this process early in your career and use it to achieve your highest possible level of success. There are several steps you can take to develop your career within an organization.

- **Explore Job Possibilities.** Find out what kind of jobs are available in your organization. Most organizations have jobs in a variety of occupations. Discover the types of jobs available by asking other workers about their jobs.

- **Identify Your Skills and Abilities.** Get to know yourself. Many of the exercises in chapter 6 helped you do this. Identify what you do best. Match these skills with jobs in the organization that require the skills you have.

- **Know Your Values.** Know what you want from your career. People define success in various ways. You may define success by your career achievements, or your job may be secondary to family, friends, recreations, etc. How much time and energy do you want to give to your job? What do you need to accomplish in your career to support your values? These are important questions to answer before setting a career goal within the company.

- **Set a Goal.** Decide on your ultimate job goal within the organization. Make sure this goal is realistic. If you want to be president of the company, are you willing to devote the time and effort required to become president? It may take you several months or a few years before you know the organization well enough to set your career or job goal.

- **Develop a Career Path.** What is the best way to advance to the position you want? There are several questions you should ask to find out:

  —What are the special qualifications needed for the job? How much experience is required? Is a license or certification necessary for the job?

  —What type of education is needed for the job? What major area of study corresponds with the job requirements? Is a college degree necessary?

  —How did other people get this job? What jobs did they have before they were promoted?

  —What type of classroom or on-the-job training is needed?

- **Write Your Plan.** Use this information to create a career plan showing the progress you want to make in the organization. Put this plan in writing. It can help motivate you to put forth more effort in reaching your goal. Include a timetable in your plan to show when you want to reach each job goal.

—**Find a Mentor.** A mentor is someone who takes a professional interest in you and advises you about your job. Ideally, a mentor should be someone who is recognized and respected in the organization. Develop a mentor relationship by asking this type of person for help on a project or for advice about a situation. You should be able to tell if this person would be willing to act as your mentor. Another approach is to ask if they are willing to mentor you. Someone who enjoys helping you is more likely to be willing to do this.

—**Keep a Record of Your Accomplishments.** The Human Resources Department and/or your supervisor probably keeps records of your work. However, don't expect them to keep a detailed record of your accomplishments. You should do this yourself. Any special skills you acquire, classes you attend, projects you complete, or ideas you suggest should be kept in a notebook or file. When you apply for promotions, use these records to help prove your qualifications.

—**Review Your Plan.** Look over your plan every six months and review your progress. If you are pleased with your rate of progress, chances are you'll be motivated to continue to work hard to reach your goal. If you are unhappy about your progress, the review can help you plan what you need to do to make better progress.

—**Change Your Plan When Necessary.** Most plans aren't perfect. Don't expect your career plan to be perfect. You will change and so will your goals. When this happens, develop a new plan. If the organization changes, it will be necessary to change your plan. You may even have to leave your current job and go to another organization to meet your goals.

Leaving a Job

There are many reasons workers leave or resign from their jobs. The reasons for resignations can be summed up in three general categories.

1. **Job Dissatisfaction.** Over time, it's possible to become unhappy with a job. Personality conflicts may occur. New management may make changes you don't feel good about. Your career plans may not work out in the business. You will know you are not satisfied if you dread going to work every day.

2. **New Opportunities.** Even though you may be happy in your job, you might be offered another job that pays more, has more opportunities for promotion, or better benefits. It is often difficult to decide what to do in these situations. However, you may very well decide to make a job change.

3. **Avoiding Disaster.** You may want to leave a job because something bad will happen if you don't. The business may close, leaving you unemployed. The company may lay you off and you can't afford to wait for a recall. It's possible you know the supervisor is unhappy with your work and is going to fire you. You you may decide to leave the job before one of these events happen.

The average person changes careers five to seven times.[3] This means there is a good chance that you will leave a job several times. It is important that you understand how to change a career the right way. Don't make errors leaving a job that you'll later regret. Here are some suggestions to help you prepare to leave a job.

- **Have Another Job Waiting.** Never leave a job without having another one available. The best time to look for a new job is when you are employed. Leaving a job to look for a job puts you at a great disadvantage. Even when you find a job, it will be harder to bargain for better pay or position if you are desperate for a paycheck.

- **Give Reasonable Notice.** The typical resignation notice is two weeks. Your employer may require a little more or less time than this. Find out from other workers the proper amount of time.

- **Be Tactful.** Don't resign in anger. You may be unhappy but it isn't a good idea to tell your supervisor what you think is wrong with the organization. You need your employer for a reference and might even want to work for your employer again some day — this is quite common. Tell the supervisor the main reason you are leaving and that you aren't angry about the situation.

- **What Are the Expectations?** Ask your supervisor what is expected during your remaining time on the job after you give your resignation. There may be forms to fill out. Often the Human Resources Department will conduct an exit interview to find out why you are leaving your job. Equipment, tools, uniforms or other items issued to you must be returned. Be sure to get a written receipt showing that you have returned the material.

- **Don't Be Disruptive.** Co-workers will wonder why you're leaving. Don't complain about your current employer to them. Let them know that you've enjoyed working with them and hope to keep in touch. Leaving a job can be sad because you often leave friends behind. If you want to be remembered as a good worker and friend, act accordingly on your last days on the job.

The most important thing about leaving a job is to be fair to both your employer and yourself. Following the guidelines above helps create a good relationship with an employer. Your employer will be happy to give you a good reference and may even rehire you in the future if you treat them fairly.

Applying What You've Learned

Read the following case studies and apply what you've learned about career development and how to leave a job.

Case Study 1

Tamara has been a clerk in the post office for five years. She recently completed a four-year degree in accounting and was offered a position with a public accounting firm. The firm wants her to start work in two weeks. Tamara must decide how to resign from her job at the post office.

1. What steps do you think Tamara should follow to resign from her current job?

_____

_____

_____

Case Study 2

Eric is very unhappy with his job. The supervisor has been giving him all the "dirty work." He has talked with his supervisor about this problem, but it hasn't helped. Eric found another job that pays better. The new employer wants him to start work immediately. Eric knows that his current employer expects at least two week's notice. However, Eric is so mad at his supervisor that he plans to call him on the phone to say he won't be in to work anymore.

1. Do you think Eric should do this? Explain the reasons for your answer.

_____

_____

_____

Summary

A job provides you with many opportunities. These opportunities include pay raises, promotions, challenges, satisfaction, recognition, friendships, and a career. It is up to you to take advantage of these opportunities. By following the suggestions in this chapter, you can reach the career goals you set for yourself. Good luck on your journey!

CONCLUSION

You have an exciting future ahead of you. Your job is an important part of that future. It provides you with the money you need to support a family, home, car, recreational activities, and other needs and interests. To support your lifestyle you must work hard at being successful in the job you have.

This workbook introduced you to the basic work skills normally required for job success. You have the ability to control your success by putting these skills into practice. Summarized this means you should:

- Know what your employer expects from you and do your best to meet those expectations.

- Be a dependable employee who is punctual and works whenever scheduled.

- Dress and groom yourself to fit into the workplace. Evening clothes and play clothes are not appropriate.

- Learn to do your job well. Take advantage of opportunities to improve your skills whenever training is offered. Be a lifelong learner.

- Believe in yourself and your abilities. Know your skills and apply them. Work to improve your weaknesses.

- Recognize the important role your supervisor plays in your job success. Listen, complete assigned tasks and volunteer to help your supervisor. Make yourself an important part of your supervisor's team.

- Cooperate and be friendly toward co-workers. Realize that working together in a group can be more successful than when each person works only for their own benefit. Your success can be built on the success of the group.

- Participate in problem solving at work. Look for problems that you can help solve. Work with your supervisor and co-workers to solve problems.

- Be an honest employee. Your employer should be able to rely on your ethical behavior.

- Know what success on the job means for you. Plan your career and know how your current job fits into your plans. If you want pay raises and promotions, know what your employer expects you to do in order to get them.

These guidelines are practical and simple to follow. Begin using them and everything else you've learned in this book. Then say to yourself: "Look out world! Here I come!"

Chapter Eleven Endnotes

1. Douglas Hall and James Goodale, *Human Resource Mangement: Strategy, Design and Implementation*, (Scott, Foresman and Company, Glenview, Ill., 1986), 490-91.

2. Arthur Sherman Jr., George Bohlander and Herbert Chruden, *Managing Human Resources*, (South-Western Publishing Co., Cincinnati, 1988), 226.

3. Michael J. Farr, *Job Finding Fast*, (Glencoe Publishing Company, Mission Hills, Calif., 1988), 13.

More Good Books from JIST Works, Inc.

JIST publishes a variety of books on careers and job search topics. Please consider ordering one or more from your dealer, local bookstore, or directly from JIST.

Orders from Individuals: Please use the form below (or provide the same information) to order additional copies of this or other books listed on this page. You are also welcome to send us your order (please enclose money order, check, or credit card information), or simply call our toll free number at **1-800-648-JIST** or **1-317-264-3720**. Our FAX number is **1-317-264-3709. Qualified schools and organizations** may request our catalog and obtain information on quantity discounts (we have over 400 career-related books, videos, and other items).

Our offices are open weekdays 8 a.m. to 5 p.m. local time and our address is:

JIST Works, Inc. • 720 North Park Avenue • Indianapolis, IN 46202-3431

QTY	BOOK TITLE	TOTAL ($)
	Getting the Job You Really Want, J. Michael Farr • ISBN: 0-942784-15-4 • **$9.95**	
	The Very Quick Job Search: Get a Good Job in Less Time, J. Michael Farr • ISBN: 0-942784-72-3 • **$9.95**	
	America's 50 Fastest Growing Jobs: An Authoritative Information Source • ISBN: 0-942784-61-8 • **$10.95**	
	America's Top 300 Jobs: A Complete Career Handbook (trade version of the *Occupational Outlook Handbook* • ISBN 0-942784-45-6 • **$17.95**	
	America's Federal Jobs: A Complete Directory of Federal Career Opportunities • ISBN 0-942784-81-2 • **$14.95**	
	The Resume Solution: How to Write and Use a Resume That Gets Results, David Swanson • ISBN 0-942784-44-8 • **$8.95**	
	The Job Doctor: Good Advice on Getting a Good Job, Phillip Norris, Ed.D. • ISBN 0-942784-43-X • **$5.95**	
	The Right Job for You: An Interactive Career Planning Guide, J. Michael Farr • ISBN 0-942784-73-1 • **$9.95**	
	Exploring Careers: A Young Person's Guide to over 300 Jobs • ISBN 0-942784-27-8 • **$19.95**	
	Work in the New Economy: Careers and Job Seeking into the 21st Century, Robert Wegmann • ISBN 0-942784-19-78 • **$14.95**	
	The Occupational Outlook Handbook • ISBN 0-942784-38-3 • **$16.95**	
	The Career Connection: Guide to College Majors and Their Related Careers, Dr. Fred Rowe • ISBN 0-942784-82-0 • **$15.95**	
	The Career Connection II: Guide to Technical Majors and Their Related Careers, Dr. Fred Rowe • ISBN 0-942784-83-9 • **$13.95**	
	Career Emphasis: Making Good Decisions • ISBN 0-942784-10-3 • **$6.95**	
	Career Emphasis: Preparing for Work • ISBN 0-942784-11-1 • **$6.95**	
	Career Emphasis: Getting a Good Job and Getting Ahead • ISBN 0-942784-13-8 • **$6.95**	
	Career Emphasis: Understanding Yourself • ISBN 0-942784-12-X • **$6.95**	
	Career & Life Skills: Making Decisions • ISBN 0-942784-57-X • **$6.95**	
	Career & Life Skills: Knowing Yourself • ISBN 0-942784-58-8 • **$6.95**	
	Career & Life Skills: Your Career • ISBN 0-942784-60-X • **$6.95**	
	Career & Life Skills: Career Preparation • ISBN 0-942784-59-6 • **$6.95**	
	Living Skills Series: Effective Communication Skills • ISBN 1-56370-038-7 942784-57-X • **$7.95**	
	Living Skills Series Why Should I Hire You? • ISBN 1-56730-039-5 • **$6.95**	
	Living Skills Series: The Two Best Ways to Find A Job • ISBN 1-56370-040-9 • **$6.95**	
	I Am (Already) Successful, Dennis Hooker • ISBN 0-942784-41-3 • **$6.95**	
	I Can Manage Life, Dennis Hooker • ISBN 0-942784-77-4 • **$8.95**	
	Young Person's Guide to Getting and Keeping a Good Job, J. Michael Farr & Marie Pavlicko • ISBN 0-942784-34-0 • **$6.95**	
	Job Savvy, LaVerne Ludden • ISBN 0-942784-79-0 • **$10.95**	

Subtotal _____

Sales Tax _____

Shipping: ($3 for first book, $1 for each additional book.) _____

(Prices subject to change without notice) (U.S. Currency only) **TOTAL ENCLOSED WITH ORDER** _____

❑ Check ❑ Money order   Credit Card: ❑ MasterCard ❑ VISA ❑ AMEX

Card # (if applies)_____ Exp. Date _____

Name (please print)_____

Name of Organization (if applies) _____

Address _____

City/State/Zip_____

Daytime Telephone (_____)_____ — _____

Thank-you for your order!